Your Florida
GOVERNMENT

ALLEN MORRIS

ANN WALDRON

Your Florida
GOVERNMENT

*500 Questions
and
Answers*

University of Florida Press   **Gainesville / 1965**

A University of Florida Press Book
IN THE
KNOW YOUR FLORIDA SERIES

Preface

IN THIS BOOK are questions people ask about Florida government—and the answers. The authors have tried to answer two general types of questions. First, we have sought to present for quick reference the questions that Florida's many new residents ask about the State government and its services and requirements—the questions about homestead exemption, automobile licenses, hunting licenses, boating licenses, and drivers' licenses.

Next, we tried to answer the questions that arise in the minds of any resident, even a native. As State government has grown bigger, it has grown more complex, and it is not difficult for the state's citizens to lose sight of the forest in the midst of all these young saplings. We have tried, therefore, to answer some of the questions that puzzled citizens have asked: Why are costs for right of way for the State Road Department so high? What is a public defender? What is the jurisdiction of the Florida Sheriffs' Bureau?

We have tried at all times to relate the questions and answers to the citizens themselves, whether they live in Pensacola, Key West, or Two Egg. This book is designed to supplement, not replace, such standard texts on State government as *The Florida Handbook*. For more detailed information about the membership of the State Legislature, for example, we refer you to other books listed in the bibliography. In this book are the answers to the questions that people have asked us, such as "Can anyone get a bill introduced in the Legislature?" and "Can anyone register as a lobbyist?"

This book is completely indexed to make it more useful as a reference book.

All questions in this book were referred to an appropriate State agency for the latest, most accurate information for the answers. Needless to say, the authors learned a lot in preparing the book. It was fun.

ALLEN MORRIS
ANN WALDRON

The Capitol
Tallahassee

Contents

CHAPTER
ONE

"We, the People
of the State of Florida . . ."

Q.—What are the five flags under which Florida has lived?
Generally, when people speak of the flags which have flown over
Florida, they are thinking of the Spanish, French, English, United
States, and Confederate. But there have been others, usually of short
duration and some of doubtful status. There was, for example, the
"Patriots' Flag" which appeared at Amelia Island during the
Spanish-American border difficulties of 1812-1819. This flag showed
a charging soldier, with fixed bayonet, and a Latin legend meaning
"Safety, the supreme law of the people."

Q.—How did Florida get its name?
Juan Ponce de León, after sighting this unknown land on April 2,
1513, named it Florida because, in the words of an ancient chronicler
of the voyage, "it appear'd very delightful, having many pleasant
groves," and also because the discovery came during *Pasqua de
Flores,* the festival of flowers held at the Easter season.

Q.—When and where was the first European settlement in Florida?
There had been a number of exploratory landings, but the first
expedition intent upon permanent colonization was put ashore at
Pensacola Bay on August 14, 1559. Under Tristán de Luna y
Arellano, there were 1,600 men and women, equipped to establish a
colony. On September 19, however, a storm destroyed the expedition's food ships. Half-starved and frustrated by an inability to get
along either with the new land or themselves, the colonists finally gave
up the struggle in the spring of 1561. The Spanish returned to
Pensacola Bay to stay in November, 1698.

Q.—Then what was the first permanent settlement in Florida?
The menace to the Spanish treasure-and-trade sea lane of a French
colony at Fort Caroline brought Crown orders to expel the French

1

and to establish a permanent Spanish defense garrison. As a consequence, Pedro Menéndez de Avilés put a Spanish fleet in at a harbor he called St. Augustine because it was August 28 (1565), the feast day of that saint. After reconnoitering the nearby coast for the French, Menéndez returned to the harbor on September 6 and disembarked troops. Their fortification of a large Indian dwelling was the beginning of St. Augustine, the oldest continuously occupied community in the present United States.

Q.—How long did the Spanish rule last?
Spain ceded Florida to England in 1763, in exchange for Havana, which the English had captured during the Seven Years' War. Spain, again at war with England, captured Pensacola in February, 1781, and thereafter controlled West Florida. East Florida was transferred back to Spain in 1783. With the exception of those years, Spanish rule lasted until the provinces of East and West Florida were ceded to the United States in 1821.

Q.—Did the French ever control all of Florida?
No. They established Fort Caroline on the St. Johns River, five miles from the sea, as a short-lived claim to interest in Florida. Beset first by hunger and then by Spaniards, Fort Caroline lasted from June 25, 1564, until mid-September, 1565. Many years afterwards, the French captured and held Pensacola, but the French area of influence always was quite limited.

Q.—When did the French give up on Florida?
France gave up on Florida in 1723 when the French returned Pensacola to Spain after having captured and occupied this community for four years.

Q.—How was Spanish Florida ruled?
The Spanish Governor was appointed by the Crown. The Council of War in Spain usually recommended three candidates to the King or Queen. The Crown selected one of the three, usually the man first on the list. The Governor was always a member of the Spanish armed forces. The Governor in reality possessed executive, legislative, and judicial authority. There was no legislative council, nor even a municipal council, in St. Augustine. Military rule prevailed. The commander of the fort was the Sergeant Major, who was responsible to the Governor. In case of the death of the Governor, the Sergeant Major became acting Governor. Outside of St. Augustine, the com-

manding authorities were the provincial Lieutenant Governors who were a part of the military garrison. [Dr. Charles W. Arnade, University of South Florida]

Q.—To whom was the Spanish Governor of Florida responsible?
In colonial Spanish administration Florida occupied a peculiar and somewhat vague and confused status. It was part of the huge Viceroyalty of New Spain, whose Viceroy resided in Mexico City. But its relation to Mexico was mostly nominal. Florida was responsible to the Audiencia of Santo Domingo. Yet the province was primarily a military outpost and military matters were of great importance; therefore, in questions of defense and related problems the Governor of Havana, who was mostly concerned with defense, had a great deal to say. All this represents a clear picture of theory, but in practice the Governor of Florida many times took matters up directly with the colonial agencies in Spain, by-passing complicated channels. In summary, Florida was the victim of an involved bureaucracy and had three superiors: Mexico City, Santo Domingo, and Havana. Sometimes she ignored them and dealt with the royal offices of the motherland. [Dr. Charles W. Arnade, University of South Florida]

Q.—How did the British get Florida?
The British won Florida at the treaty table in 1763, in exchange for Havana.

Q.—How long did British rule last?
Spain regained West Florida, by force of arms, in 1781, and was ceded East Florida in 1783. Thus, the British had possession of West Florida for approximately eighteen years, and of East Florida for twenty years.

Q.—Did the British rule Florida much as they did the colonies to the north that later became the United States?
There were Crown Governors of East and West Florida, possessed of substantially the same powers as their counterparts in the Thirteen Colonies. The Governors and the English Board of Trade aggressively promoted the Floridas both in English and in American colonial newspapers as highly desirable for land development.

Q.—Why has William Bartram's Travels *been described as "perhaps our best legacy from the English period"?*
Dr. Dorothy Dodd reports, in *Florida: the Land of Romance,* that

the young Philadelphia naturalist's record of a journey with traders in the Indian country "is one of our great nature books."

"William Bartram's poetic, yet exact, descriptions of the natural wonders of Florida have delighted generations of readers. In his own time, the English nature poets borrowed freely from his beautiful imagery.

"When Samuel Taylor Coleridge awakened one morning to set down, in 'Kubla Khan,' the lines,

" 'And there were gardens bright with sinuous rills,

Where blossom'd many an incense-bearing tree;

And here were forests ancient as the hills,

Enclosing sunny spots of greenery,'

he had been dreaming of Florida, seen through Bartram's eyes."

Q.—Why didn't Florida join the Thirteen Colonies and become part of the United States?

The colonies of East and West Florida, like the British colonies of Upper and Lower Canada, elected to remain faithful when the Continental Congress invited these two most southern and two most northern colonies to join with the other thirteen. Dr. Rembert W. Patrick says the reasons for refusal by the Floridas were obvious: "The colonies were young and tied to the Mother Country; they needed her protection against the Indians and England's economic aid; and their people were satisfied and had few connections with the colonies to the north. Furthermore, the non-British residents of the Floridas—Minorcans, French, Greek, Italians, and Spaniards— had no desire to be associated with the Protestant peoples of the other English southern colonies."

Q.—Did the United States buy Florida?

The United States assumed liability for claims of its citizens against Spain up to $5 million. It did not pay any money directly to Spain. [State Librarian]

Q.—When Florida was a Territory, how was it governed?

The Territory of Florida was governed by a governor, appointed by the President, and a Legislative Council of thirteen citizens of the Territory. From 1822 to 1825 the council members were appointed by the President. Thereafter, they were elected by the people of the Territory.

Q.—Who was the first Territorial Governor of Florida?

Andrew Jackson, afterwards President of the United States, was appointed on March 10, 1821, as United States Commissioner exercising all the powers formerly possessed by the Spanish governors of East and West Florida. The unified Territory of Florida was established March 30, 1822, and William P. DuVal of Kentucky was commissioned on April 17, 1822, as Governor. Between the time that Jackson left Florida, probably on October 8, 1821, and Governor DuVal's arrival on June 20, 1822, Territorial Secretaries administered the government of Florida.

Q.—How did Tallahassee—"way up there"—get to be the capital of the State?

The land occupied now by Tallahassee was chosen in 1823 as the seat of government for the newly formed American Territory of Florida. It was selected by commissioners appointed to locate a new capital between the old Spanish (and English) territorial capitals of St. Augustine and Pensacola. Of course, Tallahassee was not "way up there" in terms of population at the time, for the peninsula was sparsely inhabited.

Q.—How did the Seminole Tribes begin?

As Wyatt Blassingame remarks in his *Seminoles of Florida,* "a great deal of Seminole history is open to controversy." At least three Indian tribes were found in Florida by the Spanish explorers, but these had been largely exterminated by 1700. Other Indians then began to move into Florida, mostly from tribes of the Creek Confederacy. An early Indian agent, reports Blassingame, explained that the word "Seminole" meant "runaway" or "broken off." Therefore, the name was applicable to the Indians in the Territory of Florida "since most of them ran away from the Creek Nation." These Indians from the North, plus remnants of the ancient Florida tribes, gradually evolved into the Seminoles. Yet it should be remembered that the Seminoles still are not a single tribe. There are Miccosukee and Muskogee groups.

Q.—How did the Seminole War end? Who won?

No clear-cut victory was won by either the United States or the Seminoles. Each may be said to have worn the other out. Finally, the Civil War provided a diversion which enabled both sides in Florida to adjust to the other's presence. Meanwhile, in the struggle which began in 1835, nearly all of the Indians had been transported to Arkansas or had died as a consequence either of the fighting or the trip. The federal government had lost some 1,600 men and spent

upwards of $50 million. This judgment is passed by Marjory Stone-
man Douglas in her book, *The Everglades: River of Grass*: "It was
war in which only the resistance and determination of the Indians,
not four thousand people all told, against the whole might of the
United States of America, could be called heroic."

*Q.—Is it true that the Seminoles are still at war with the United
    States?*
Wyatt Blassingame says that the question of whether the Seminoles
are still theoretically at war, never having signed a peace treaty, is
the one most often asked at the Dania Agency of the United States
Indian Service. The answer, continues Blassingame, is Yes, but this
"is now due more to Federal law than to Seminole irreconcilability."
In 1871 Congress passed an act stating: "No Indian tribe or nation
within the territory of the United States shall be acknowledged or
recognized as an independent nation, tribe, or power, with whom
the United States may contract by treaty."

Q.—Did the people of Florida vote to become a state?
Florida was admitted to the Union by an act of Congress approved
by President John Tyler on March 3, 1845. No referendum was held
on that act, but the people of Florida had voted 2,214 to 1,274 in
1837 in favor of becoming a state. A convention was held at St.
Joseph in 1838-1839 to draft a constitution in preparation for statehood. Congress, committed by the Missouri Compromise to admitting
states in pairs from the North and South, delayed Florida's entrance
to the Union until Iowa was ready in 1845.

Q.—Is it "Floridian" or "Floridan"?
Either is correct, but "Floridian" is much the more general in today's
usage. William Roberts, in 1763, wrote of the "longevity of the Floridan Indians." William Bartram, in 1791, said "the Creeks subdued
the remnant tribes of the ancient Floridans." During this same period, Jonathan Carver, in 1778, reported that "I must exclude the
stories he has introduced of the Huron and Floridan women." The
Oxford English Dictionary says of "-ian" (meaning "of" or "be-
longing to") that the suffix forms both the adjective and substantive
in "modern formations from proper names, the number of which is
without limit."

Q.—Who are Floridians?
Only 36 per cent of the 1960 population of Florida were born in the

state, according to the report of the United States Bureau of the Census. Making up the 64 per cent born elsewhere are: 15 per cent from the northeastern states, 12.3 per cent from the north-central states, 25.8 per cent from other southern states, 5.5 per cent from foreign countries, 1.2 per cent from western states, 0.3 per cent from outlying U. S. possessions (Puerto Rico, Virgin Islands, etc.), 0.3 per cent born abroad or at sea, and 3.6 per cent who gave no place of origin. [Development Commission]

Q.—What is the nickname of Floridians?
Floridians are known as "crackers," but the nickname should be used with care. Its acceptance by Floridians depends upon the person and, in some measure, upon the section of the state. A historian illustrated this shading by saying that if, while out of the state, some-one hailed her as a cracker, she would respond affirmatively. If, however, someone in Florida described her as a cracker, she would want to think it over. A number of origins are suggested. Francis R. Goulding, in *Marooner's Island* (1869), thought the name was de-rived from Scotch settlers in whose dialect a "cracker" was a person who talked boastingly. John Lambert, in *Travels Through Lower Canada, and the United States of North America* (1810), wrote: "The waggoners are familiarly called *crackers* (from the smacking of their whip, I suppose)." Emily P. Burke, in *Reminiscences of Georgia* (1850), said crackers were called that "from the circum-stance that they formerly pounded all their corn, which is their prin-cipal article of diet." Two modern historians, A. J. and Kathryn Abbey Hanna, writing in their *Lake Okeechobee* (1948), said: "The name 'cracker' frequently applied to countrymen of Georgia and Florida is supposed to have originated as a cattle term." Florida cowboys popped whips of braided buckskin, twelve to eighteen feet long. The "crack" sounded like a rifle shot and at times could be heard for several miles. The writer of the newspaper column "Cracker Politics" suggests it might be prudent to accompany the nickname with a smile.

Q.—How was the first State Legislature apportioned?
The first State Legislature was apportioned by the Constitution of 1839, with a Senate of 16 districts and 17 Senators (Leon County had 2) and a House of Representatives of 41 Members (with a ceiling of 60 after future reapportionments).

Q.—Is it true that legislators from Key West used to have to go to New York by boat and then come to Tallahassee?

It is possible there may have been some instances of this. However, it seems more likely that Key West legislators would have boarded ships on the frequent sailings from there to nearer Gulf ports: Apalachicola, St. Marks, and Pensacola being among these. Certainly there were ships to Savannah and Charleston if the necessity existed for going beyond Florida.

Q.—Were Floridians pretty well unanimous in their sympathy for the Confederate cause?

If opinion may be determined from public expression in the short campaign for election of delegates to the Secession Convention of January, 1861, the issue was immediate withdrawal from the Union as against cooperation with other southern states contemplating such action. Dr. Dorothy Dodd, writing the history of those days, says: "Only a few voices were raised against secession under any and all circumstances. Former Governor Richard K. Call stood almost alone when he protested that secession was nothing short of treason." Some 16,000 Floridians served in the armed forces during the War Between the States: 15,000 in the Confederate service and 1,290 in the Union army.

Q.—Did Florida make any important contributions to the Confederate cause?

In addition to the 15,000 men in the armed forces, Florida contributed foodstuffs—beef, salt, pork, sugar, syrup, and fish—to the Confederate war effort.

Q.—Was Florida occupied by federal troops after the War Between the States?

Florida civil officers were subject to the military authority of the District of Florida from the end of the war until March, 1867, when the state was placed under military rule by the first Reconstruction Act. At the inauguration of Governor Harrison Reed, July 4, 1868, Colonel John T. Sprague relinquished his authority as Military and Civil Governor of Florida to Governor Reed, but federal troops were stationed in the state until 1877. [State Librarian]

Q.—Did Florida have a Negro government during Reconstruction?

No. A number of Negroes served in the Legislature during Reconstruction but no Negro was ever governor, and only one, Jonathan C.

Gibbs, served as a member of the Cabinet. Gibbs served as Secretary of State (1868-1872) and as State Superintendent of Public Instruction (1873-1874). [State Librarian]

Q.—Who designed our State flag?
The basic design of the State flag was suggested by the Committee on Miscellaneous Articles of the Constitutional Convention of 1868, of which Simon B. Conover was chairman. The committee's proposal that the flag should consist of a white field upon which was impressed the Great Seal of the State became a part of the Constitution of 1868, and was continued in the present constitution. The addition of diagonal red bars by constitutional amendment in 1900 was suggested by former Governor Francis P. Fleming, who had noted that when a flag with a white field "hung limp to the staff," it gave the appearance of being a flag of truce. [State Librarian]

Q.—Did Florida ever approve the Fourteenth Amendment to the Constitution of the United States—the so-called "equal rights" amendment?
The Florida Legislature refused to ratify the Fourteenth Amendment in 1866, by unanimous vote of each house. After the Reconstruction Act of March 2, 1867, made ratification a condition to readmission to the Union, the Legislature ratified the amendment on June 9, 1868, by a vote of 23 to 6 in the Assembly and of 10 to 3 in the Senate. As a result of this action, Florida's congressmen were seated on June 25. Since the state was under military rule until July 4, a bill ratifying the Amendment a second time was passed by the Senate on July 27, by the Assembly on July 29, and approved by the Governor on July 31. [State Librarian]

Q.—Where is the original copy of the State Constitution?
The original handwritten copy of the present State Constitution, adopted in 1885, is in the office of the Secretary of State in Tallahassee. [Secretary of State]

Q.—What is the Preamble to the State Constitution?
A preamble states the purpose of the people in agreeing to a constitution. In its entirety, the Preamble to the Constitution of Florida says: "We, the people of the State of Florida, being grateful to Almighty God for our constitutional liberty, in order to secure its benefits, form a more perfect government, insure domestic tranquility, maintain public order, and guarantee equal civil and political rights to all, do

ordain and establish this constitution." While this Preamble was adopted by the Legislature in 1961 and by the voters the following year, the language follows closely the original wording of 1885. The new Preamble was intended to give more pleasing grammatical form to the old ideals.

Q.—How can I get a copy of the State Constitution?
By writing to the Secretary of State, Tallahassee. There is no charge.

Q.—Why do states have to keep rewriting their constitutions when the federal Constitution stays basically the same? The United States Constitution has been amended but states frequently adopt new constitutions. Why?

During the course of our national history, the fifty states have had 134 constitutions, excluding the Constitution of Puerto Rico adopted in 1952. These documents have been amended thousands of times; more than 3,000 amendments have been added to the state constitutions now in effect. In great contrast, there are only 24 amendments to the Constitution of the United States, including the recently ratified Poll Tax Amendment. Of these, the first ten were added at the same time in the early 1790's.

The Constitution of the United States, unlike most state constitutions, is confined in most of its provisions to fundamental matters. It is framed in general terms, thus providing the flexibility that has enabled it to be adapted to changing problems and needs of a dynamic society. Its adaptability, through amendments and interpretation by the judiciary as well as the legislative and executive branches, is the principal reason for the survival of the national document.

The contents of most state constitutions, including the present Constitution of Florida, are more parochial, detailed, and reflective of specific problems, needs, trends, and thoughts of the times in which they are drawn. They are far less flexible than the national instrument and far less adaptable to new problems. If you study the amendments to the present Florida Constitution, you will note that their number and frequency has increased in recent decades, affording at least some evidence of the growing inadequacy of this document to fulfill our burgeoning needs. [Dr. Albert L. Sturm, Director, Institute of Governmental Research, the Florida State University]

Q.—Why are there cannons on the front steps of the Capitol?
These cannons, dating back to 1863, are relics of the Civil War. They

were found in the vicinity of Tallahassee and were placed on the front steps of the Capitol to commemorate the successful defense at the Battle of Natural Bridge of the only Confederate capital east of the Mississippi River not occupied during the war by Union forces. [Secretary of State]

Q.—Is the Capitol Building open to visitors at all times?
No. The Capitol Building is open from 8:00 A. M. to midnight every day of the year, including holidays. On Monday through Friday, guides are available from eight to five. [Secretary of State]

Q.—Since "capitol" means the building and "capital" the city, isn't "Capitol Building" needlessly tautological?
Pedantically, perhaps. Since the development of the Capitol Center, with State agencies housed in numerous buildings ringing the Capitol, it has become the custom to speak of the "Capitol Building" so that there is no doubt which structure is actually meant. It is true that this occurs usually in conversation. Incidentally, those who drafted the Constitution in 1885, in detailing the duties of the Secretary of State, wrote he "shall also have charge of the Capitol building and grounds. . . ."

Q.—What was the first lighthouse in Florida?
It is not possible to pinpoint this with exactness, as it might be said that a lantern displayed from a building on some Florida shore could have been used as a signal to mariners. The oldest Florida lighthouse, built as such and still operated, is at St. Augustine. The Coast Guard says the St. Augustine lighthouse was established in 1824. It was rebuilt in 1874, now stands 161 feet above the water, and has the strength of 450,000 candles. The Pensacola and Key West lighthouses were established in 1825. Pensacola's was rebuilt in 1858, stands 191 feet above water, and has a candle power of 3,000,000. Key West's was rebuilt in 1846, stands 91 feet above water, and has a candle power of 50,000.

Q.—What are states' rights?
Historically, "states' rights" are the rights reserved to the states, under the United States Constitution, to regulate the domestic affairs of their citizens, as contrasted with the right of the federal government to regulate foreign affairs and those domestic affairs which cannot effectively be regulated by a state acting independently of others. [Farris Bryant, as Governor, 1964]

Q.—Do the State Archives have any important documents on file?
Florida does not now possess State Archives in the sense of a museum-type building and a staff for the collection and display of documents and other objects of patriotic, historical, and general interest. The Secretary of State, as the recording officer for the State government, has some objects of substantial historical value in his office at the Capitol: for example, the original of the 1885 Constitution. The Strozier Library at the Florida State University at Tallahassee houses the state's Photographic Archives, with a systematic, continuing effort to document in pictures the development of Florida and Floridians since photography became known in the state about the time of the Civil War. The State Library and Historical Commission has legal authority for collecting archives but little money and little space for doing this.

The State Library at Tallahassee has, however, as fine a collection of ephemeral Floridiana—advertising pamphlets and similar short-lived but revealing material—as can be found anywhere. At the University of Florida in Gainesville, the P. K. Yonge Library of Florida History may be regarded as *the* repository of the state's newspapers. These are there in original and microfilm from the earliest days of Florida journalism until the present.

There is reason to believe that Florida has reached that phase of a state's evolution when its people begin to take more interest in the preservation and documentation of the past and present. Florida once was described as "an old land of new people," because so many of its people were born elsewhere. These people tended to think of their state heritage as being elsewhere. Slowly that tendency is changing.

Q.—How did the Everglades get their name?
Marjory Stoneman Douglas wrote the book, *The Everglades: River of Grass,* which explores this unique region. She says that Spanish mapmakers, who never saw the Everglades, printed the words "El Laguno del Espíritu Santo" on this unknown space. An English surveyor, who may have looked out over the endless, watery expanse, called them "River Glades" on his map. On later maps, "River" became "Ever." Mrs. Douglas goes on to say that the present name came into general use only after the acquisition of Florida from Spain in 1819. Yet even so late as 1856, maps carried the words "Ever" and "Glades" separately, and the text did not give them the capitalization of a proper name. The word "glade" is derived from the

Anglo-Saxon "glæd," meaning "shining" or "bright." In England, says Mrs. Douglas, for more than a thousand years the word "glæd," and then "glade," has meant an open green grassy place in the forest. Incidentally, the Indians called them "Pa-hay-okee," or "Grassy Water." "Today," writes Mrs. Douglas, "Everglades is one word and yet plural. They are the only Everglades in the world."

Q.—What is the State tree?
The Sabal palm (*Sabal palmetto*) was designated the State tree by the 1953 Legislature. After controversy stretching over a number of legislative sessions, the 1953 Legislature adopted the view of the Florida Federation of Garden Clubs that palms are characteristic of Florida and that of the palms, the Sabal was most widely distributed in the state.

Q.—What is the State song?
Stephen Collins Foster's *Old Folks at Home,* which in Florida is better known, from its first line, as "Way down upon de Swanee ribber." The 1935 Legislature decreed its use, and the State has erected a memorial to Foster on the Suwannee at White Springs. This memorial draws thousands of visitors annually to its museum, with wonderfully contrived dioramas, and to its bell tower and other attractions.

Q.—What is the State bird?
The mockingbird, designated by the 1927 Legislature.

Q.—What is the State flower?
The orange blossom, so declared by the 1909 Legislature.

The Governor, the Cabinet, and the System

Q.—What is the Cabinet?

By usage, the members of the Cabinet are the top executive officers of Florida's state government. When people in government speak of the Cabinet, they mean the six officers who can be re-elected. They exclude the Governor, who ordinarily cannot be elected for a successive term.

The Constitution refers to this group of six as "the administrative officers of the Executive Department." These are (in the order they are listed in the Constitution) the Secretary of State, Attorney General, Comptroller, Treasurer, Superintendent of Public Instruction, and Commissioner of Agriculture.

Nowhere in the Constitution does the word "cabinet" appear except in section headings unofficially supplied by the Secretary of State. The Constitution says "the Supreme Executive power of the State shall be vested in a Chief Magistrate, who shall be styled the Governor of Florida." (The capitalization is that of the Constitution.) Thereafter, the Constitution says "the governor shall be assisted by administrative officers as follows"—naming the Cabinet members.

In recent years, newsmen have referred to the Cabinet as though the Governor were a member. Thus, "Cabinet" has become the Tallahassee reporter's shorthand for the various boards on which the Governor and the independent executive officers serve. When the Board of Commissioners of State Institutions (composed of the Governor and all six Cabinet members) takes some action, the newsmen are likely to report "the Cabinet today" did thus and so. But old Capitol hands may say "the Board of Commissioners" when talking about the same action.

14

Q.—Why is the Cabinet system often described as unique?
In Florida, not only the Governor but all six members of the administrative family are elected. As suggested in the preceding answer, it is important to remember that this is not "the Governor's Cabinet" but the "Governor and the Cabinet." Each member is fully independent in the sense of having been elected by the people to manage separate departments of the State government.

Keeping in mind the fact that the Governor and the members of the Cabinet possess individual authority over specific departments of the government, the same officers—all or some of them—sit also as members of numerous boards which transact much of the State's business. As members of the Budget Commission, they control the release of all the money appropriated by the Legislature, at times reducing the sums. Or, as members of the Board of Commissioners of State Institutions, they manage the prisons and hospitals for the mentally ill and the retarded. And, as Trustees of the Internal Improvement Fund, they oversee the State's land holdings. And so on, through many other changes of hat by the same people.

This arrangement has been described by political scientists as a "collegial executive," or government by a body of persons having common functions. From one point of view, it represents a proliferation within the executive department of the checks-and-balances which usually separate the legislative, executive, and judicial branches of a government.

It means that the Governor may have to clear through the Cabinet some project on which he campaigned for election. He well may chafe at this restraint. Usually this occurs in the early days of a gubernatorial administration, for no amount of book reading or even legislative experience ever seems to equip a new Governor for the facts of Cabinet life. So much public attention is given campaigns for Governor that the new chief executive thinks of himself as boss. But when he seats himself at the board table, he is one among equals in the disposition of matters which are board responsibilities. On the boards, each member has one vote and the majority rules. Hence, the Governor can be out-voted and sometimes is.

But there is another aspect of Cabinet administration. Once, while juggling a politically awkward problem, a Governor privately applauded the system as a device for "spreading the heat." He meant the board method resulted in a diffusion of responsibility which relieved him of the burden of being singled out as the officer making a decision which would be unpopular with some. It's hard to quarrel with a board.

Too, when the new Governor seats himself at the board table, his colleagues generally will possess the advantage of having been there before he arrived and he knows most of them will be there after he's gone. This could be a humbling thought.

Q.—Does the Governor appoint the Cabinet?
No, except in the case of a vacancy. The members of the Cabinet are elected at the same time as the voting for Governor. Regularly, the members of the Cabinet serve four-year terms, but, unlike the Governor, they may be re-elected—and usually are.

Q.—When does the Cabinet meet?
By custom, the Cabinet (including the Governor as Chairman) meets each Tuesday in the Boardroom of the Office of the Governor. In succession, the executive officers meet as members of the various boards, changing swiftly from one board to another with the completion of the business of each. The onlooker will be aware of the change largely because the staff for one board will leave the big board table and that of another will slip into the vacated places.

Q.—Can anyone attend a Cabinet meeting?
Yes. Meetings of the various boards are almost invariably open to the public, and seats are provided for visitors. Beginning in the 1940's, "executive," or closed, meetings became less frequent, and nowadays there are virtually none.

Q.—Who decides ultimately how much each State agency will spend?
That depends on what is meant by "ultimately." Each agency calculates its needs. The Budget Commission (composed of the Governor and the Cabinet) reviews those requests and makes a recommendation to the Legislature. The separate Committees on Appropriations of the Legislature then review the agency requests and the Budget Commission recommendations, and may independently interview officers of the agencies. After the Senate and House committees have reported out their versions, the general membership will have an opportunity to offer amendments either raising or reducing specific items. But the "ultimate" decision on how much an agency will receive (within the total appropriated by the Legislature and not vetoed by the Governor) will be made by the Budget Commission on

the basis of revenue collections. The Budget Commission has been empowered by the Legislature to release money to agencies by quarters, thus enabling the Budget Commission to react promptly to fluctuations in tax collections. Since the Legislature appropriates for a two-year period, this flexibility in releases is desirable.

Q.—Can the Budget Commission withhold appropriated funds unless there is an actual cash shortage?

Yes. The discretion vested by the Legislature in the Budget Commission is quite broad. There are a number of reasons for this. As a matter of unwritten policy, the Legislature usually appropriates more money than estimates of tax revenue indicate for the two years ahead. This over-appropriating is in the nature of a gamble and, since the State government can spend only dollars actually in hand, no real harm is done.

Why does the Legislature appropriate more money than estimates indicate will be available? In the first place, conditions may prove more favorable than appeared at the time the revenue estimates were made. There may be tax windfalls. The Estate Tax, for example, may yield far more money than was expected, by reason of the death of more than the usual number of wealthy Floridians.

Too, appropriations are based on such things as welfare case loads, hospital patient loads, and college student enrollments. These are estimates. The demand may fall short in actuality of the numbers estimated by administrators, who may be expected to guess on the safe, or high, side. The Budget Commission holds the releases to the sum actually required.

The Legislature occasionally will go along with a lawmaker's request to approve an appropriation for some State purpose, usually in the capital outlay category, with the understanding that the money will not be released until all other needs have been satisfied. These second priority appropriations may never be released during the biennium covered by the General Appropriations Law. But the sponsor of, say, a new State park, will feel that its inclusion in a law at one session will earn the proposed park a higher rating at the next session.

These, then, are some of the reasons why the Legislature appropriates more money than its own revenue analysts foresee, and why the Budget Commission has the authority to control spending.

In reality, the Governor's veto of appropriations has been used less and less because his purpose can be better achieved through the Budget Commission. (He is Chairman of the Budget Commission.) A veto strikes out an entire item, killing it completely. The Budget Commission either can put the item on the shelf, a softer way of accomplishing the same result, or if money becomes available during the two years after the Legislature goes home, an amount less than the appropriated sum may be released. In effect, therefore, the appropriation can be reduced.

Q.—Does the Budget Commission make a budget for all State expenditures?
Yes. The Commission prepares this budget for the Legislature by requiring requests for funds, with justifications in writing, from all State agencies. These requests are required from the agencies by November 15, for the two-year operating period beginning the following July 1.

Q.—Has a Cabinet member ever become Governor?
Yes. Governor Park Trammell (1913-1917) had been a member of the Cabinet as Attorney General (1909-1913). Governor William D. Bloxham (1881-1885, 1897-1901) had been a member as Secretary of State (1877-1880) and as Comptroller (1890-1897).

Q.—What does the Governor do?
The duties of a Governor fall into three broad categories: (1) to discharge the responsibilities imposed upon him as an individual officer by the Constitution and the laws; (2) to serve, usually with all or some members of the Cabinet, upon numerous ex-officio boards; and (3) to perform what might be described as the implied obligations of the office.

The Governor's constitutional and statutory duties include these: To exercise the supreme executive power of the state and to take care that the laws be faithfully executed. To approve or disapprove acts which have been passed by the Legislature, with authority to disapprove specific items within acts making appropriations. To convene the Legislature in special session, and to adjourn the Legislature in the event of disagreement between the houses as to the time of adjournment. To give the Legislature information on the state of government and to recommend expedient measures. To sign all commissions issued in the name of the State. To serve as commander in chief of the State militia, and to appoint all commissioned officers of the State's units of the National Guard. To fill vacancies in the United States Senate. To grant reprieves and suspend fines in all cases except impeachment. To appoint on his own initiative, or with the advice and consent of the Senate, officials specified in the statutes and Constitution. To suspend from office, for cause, all elective and appointive officers not subject to impeachment. By and with the consent of the Senate, such suspended officers may be removed. To act as needed in all matters of extradition of persons charged with crime. To proclaim holidays. To countersign all warrants for payment of State funds.

The Governor serves as a member (and, usually by custom and sometimes by designation in the Constitution or law, as Chairman) of the following boards: Board of Administration, Armory Board, Boating Council, Bond Review Board, Budget Commission, Civil Defense Council, Board of Conservation, Board of Drainage Commissioners, Board of Education, Housing Board, Inter-American Center Authority, Trustees of the Internal Improvement Fund, Labor Business Agents Licensing Board, Outdoor Recreational Development Council, Outdoor Recreational Planning Committee, Pardon Board, Pension Board, Personnel Board, Executive Board of the Department of Public Safety, Purchasing Commission, Revenue Commission, Sheriffs' Bureau, Board of Commissioners of State Institutions, Board of Trustees of Teacher Retirement Fund, Textbook Purchasing Board, Vocational Education Board.

The implied obligations include the giving of leadership in matters of a community nature, such as a campaign to reduce traffic deaths through urging motorists to drive more carefully. Too, these implied obligations require him to represent the State in a ceremonial way. This could be done, for example, through welcoming conventions, attending expositions, and traveling outside Florida to attract tourists and industries.

Q.—What does the Secretary of State do?
As do those of the Governor, the duties of the Secretary of State fall into three areas of activity: (1) to carry out the duties imposed upon him by the Constitution and laws; (2) to serve on various of the ex-officio boards provided to give leadership in specific governmental fields; and (3) to perform the ceremonial duties which have devolved upon the Secretary of State by custom.

The Secretary of State's constitutional and statutory duties include these: To supervise state elections, to charter corporations, to license labor business agents and private employment agencies, to register trademarks, to commission notaries public. To be custodian of documents of state, including original copies of laws, the journals of the House and Senate, and the Florida Constitution. To be custodian of the Great Seal of the State of Florida and the State flag. To record and countersign commissions, proclamations, and directives of the Governor. To be custodian of the Capitol Building and grounds.

The Secretary of State serves as a member (and, usually by custom, as Vice-Chairman) of the following boards: Budget Commission, Board of State Canvassers, Civil Defense Council, Board of Conservation, Board of Education, Labor Business Agents Licensing Board, Outdoor Recreational Development Council, Pardon Board, Personnel Board, Public Records Screening Board, Executive Board of the Department of Public Safety, Purchasing Commission, Revenue Commission, Board of Commissioners of State Institutions, Board of Trustees of the Teacher Retirement Fund, Textbook Purchasing Board, Vocational Education Board.

The Secretary of State, along with the Governor and the other members of the Cabinet, represents official Florida by participation in a multiplicity of public functions. He may address a college commencement, preside at the opening of a new mental hospital, or serve at a national waterways conference.

Q.—What does the Attorney General do?
In common with the Governor and the other members of the Cabinet, the Attorney General functions in three areas of activity. (See prefaces to description of the duties of the Governor and the Secretary of State.)

The Attorney General's constitutional and statutory duties include these: To serve as legal advisor of the Governor and other Executive Officers of the State, and State agencies. To defend the public interests. To represent the State in legal proceedings. To keep a record of his official acts and opinions. To index statutes and resolutions of each session of the Legislature. To serve as a reporter for the Supreme Court. To conduct a continuing study of statutes for revision and improvement. To assemble the Circuit Judges in biennial session to consider the betterment of the judicial system, including recommendations for legislation. To report to the Governor, for transmission to the Legislature, on the operation of laws of the last previous session, including decisions of the courts affecting these laws.

In addition to these duties, it has been held by our State Supreme Court that the duties and powers of the Attorney General include the duties and powers exercised by the Attorney General as chief legal advisor of the King under the common law of England. Thus, the Attorney General may engage upon matters affecting the public interest, even though such engagement is not specifically provided for by statutory law.

The Attorney General serves as a member of the following boards: Boating Council, Budget Commission, Board of Canvassers, Civil Defense Council, Board of Conservation, County Officers Budget Appeals, Board of Drainage Commissioners, Board of Education, Housing Board, Trustees of Internal Improvement Fund, Interstate Cooperation Commission, Board for Fixing Values of Investment Securities of Trust Companies, Judicial Council, Outdoor Recreational Development Council, Pardon Board, Personnel Board, Public Records Screening Board, Executive Board of the Department of Public Safety, Purchasing Commission, Railroad Assessment Board, Revenue Commission, Securities Commission, Sheriffs' Bureau, Board of Commissioners of State Institutions, Board for Supervision of Form of Bond of Surety Companies, Board of Trustees of Teacher Retirement Fund, Textbook Purchasing Board, Vocational Education Board.

Q.—What does the Comptroller do?
In common with the Governor and the other members of the Cabinet, the Comptroller functions in three areas of activity. (See prefaces to description of the duties of the Governor and Secretary of State.)

The Comptroller's constitutional and statutory duties include these: To pre-audit all claims against the State. To issue warrants for the payment of salaries and claims. To record all revenues collected, disbursements, and appropriation balances. To supervise banks, trust companies, building and loan associations, credit unions, and small loan companies. To administer the affairs of closed banking institutions. To collect estate, documentary stamp, utilities, and occupational license taxes. To supervise the collection of intangible tax information for county assessors. To administer the State and County Officers' Retirement System. To certify amounts due counties under the school minimum foundation program.

The Comptroller serves as a member of the following boards: Board of Administration, Bond Review Board, Budget Commission, Board of Canvassers, Board of Conservation, Board of Drainage Commission, Housing Board, Board of Trustees of the Internal Improvement Fund, Board for Fixing Values of Investment Securities of Trust Companies, Outdoor Recreational Development Council, Pardon Board, Pension Board, Personnel Board, Executive Board of the Department of Public Safety, Purchasing Commission, Railroad Assessment Board, Revenue Commission, Securities Commission, Board of Commissioners of State Institutions, Board for Supervision of Form of Bond of Surety Companies, Textbook Purchasing Board.

Q.—What does the Treasurer do?

In common with the Governor and the other members of the Cabinet, the Treasurer functions in three areas of activity. (See prefaces to description of the duties of the Governor and the Secretary of State.)

The Treasurer's constitutional and statutory duties include these: To pay warrants drawn on the Treasurer and keep detailed records. To deposit State funds in banks, requiring collateral as security. To serve as Treasurer of the State Board of Administration. To serve as custodian for all State-owned securities. As State Fire Marshal, to investigate suspicious fires. To promulgate and enforce safety regulations, controlling storage, sale, and use of liquefied petroleum gas, combustibles, and explosives. As State Insurance Commissioner, to supervise insurance companies and their agents and adjusters, and collect the State's tax on insurance. To enforce the Motor Vehicle Financial Responsibility Law. To approve organization of non-profit hospitalization associations.

The Treasurer serves as a member of the following boards: Board of Administration, Bond Review Board, Budget Commission, Civil Defense Council, Board of Conservation, Board of Drainage Commissioners, Board of Education, Finance Committee, Housing Board, Board of Trustees of the Internal Improvement Fund, Board for Fixing Values of Investment Securities of Trust Companies, Outdoor Recreational Planning Council, Pension Board, Personnel Board, Executive Board of the Department of Public Safety, Purchasing Commission, Railroad Assessment Board, Revenue Commission, Securities Commission, State and County Officers and Employees Retirement Trust Investment Board, Board of Commissioners of State Institutions, Board for Supervision of Form of Bond of

Surety Companies, Board of Trustees of the Teacher Retirement Fund, Textbook Purchasing Board, Board of Vocational Education.

Q.—What does the Superintendent of Public Instruction do?
In common with the Governor and other members of the Cabinet, the Superintendent of Public Instruction functions in three areas of activity. (See prefaces to description of the duties of the Governor and the Secretary of State.)

The Superintendent of Public Instruction's constitutional and statutory duties include these: To exercise general supervision over education in public elementary and secondary schools and junior colleges. To recommend to the State Board of Education policies for school betterment. To act as Secretary and Executive Officer of the State Board of Education. To apportion all State school funds among the counties. To exercise supervision over county school budgets, and approve or recommend changes in these. To issue to qualified applicants teacher certificates, permits, and licenses authorized by law, and to recommend revocation of these for cause. To recommend policies for the preservation of the principal of the State Permanent School Fund. To recommend and execute plans for cooperation with the federal government for the conduct of a vocational education and rehabilitation program in the state. To prepare and recommend to the Board of Education minimum standards and rules and regulations in the following fields: establishment, organization, operation, and classification of schools; personnel; child welfare; courses of study and instructional aids; transportation; school plant, finance, and records and reports. To serve as ex-officio Secretary and keep the records of the State Advisory Council on Education. To assist County Boards in purchase of school buses, equipment, and supplies by providing a plan whereby bids therefor may be pooled.

The Superintendent of Public Instruction serves as a member of the following boards: Commission on Aging, Budget Commission, Civil Defense Council, Board of Conservation, Board of Education, Higher Education Facilities Act Advisory Committee, Labor Business Agents Licensing Board, Outdoor Recreational Development Council, Personnel Board, Executive Board of the Department of Public Safety, Purchasing Commission, Revenue Commission, Board of Commissioners of State Institutions, Board of Trustees of Teachers Retirement Fund, Textbook Purchasing Board, Vocational Education Board.

Q.—What does the Commissioner of Agriculture do?

In common with the Governor and other members of the Cabinet, the Commissioner of Agriculture functions in three areas of activity. (See prefaces to description of duties of the Governor and the Secretary of State.)

The Commissioner of Agriculture's constitutional and statutory duties include these: To give leadership to the State's services to agriculture. To administer laws enacted for the health and welfare of consumers of farm and related products. To inspect fertilizers, feeds, seeds, petroleum products, frozen desserts, pesticides, fruits, vegetables, and milk products. To collect and disseminate agricultural information. To administer the Department of Agriculture.

The Commissioner of Agriculture serves as a member of the following boards: Budget Commission, Civil Defense Council, Board of Conservation, Board of Drainage Commissioners, Housing Board, Board of Trustees of Internal Improvement Fund, Outdoor Recreational Development Council, Pardon Board, Personnel Board, Executive Board of the Department of Public Safety, Purchasing Commission, Revenue Commission, Board of Commissioners of State Institutions, Textbook Purchasing Board.

Q.—What is the Little Cabinet?

The term "Little Cabinet" has been applied by custom, not law, to the group of officials heading agencies regarded as extensions of the Governor's own office. Membership in this group varies from administration to administration, but generally speaking the Little Cabinet is composed of the Chairman of the Road Department, the Chairman of the Industrial Commission, the Chairman of the Development Commission, the Chairman of the Racing Commission, the Chairman of the Turnpike Authority, the Motor Vehicle Commissioner, the Hotel and Restaurant Commissioner, and the Beverage Director. The Executive Assistant to the Governor is also a member of the Little Cabinet. These are the officers who are brought into the State government by the new Governor and usually leave when he does.

Q.—All right, now there are in the executive branch the Governor, the Cabinet, and the Little Cabinet. Where do the Director of Public Safety, Conservation Director, and Prisons Director fit into the picture?

The Director of the Department of Public Safety, the Director of the Board of Conservation, and the Director of the Division of Corrections for the Board of Commissioners of State Institutions are the administrators employed by those Cabinet boards. While they hold positions of importance, they are not, strictly speaking, "officers." Along with their counterparts in other Cabinet agencies, these administrators are employees, each of whom serves at the pleasure of his own board. It should be added, however, that these administrators usually enjoy long tenure.

Q.—What are the "administrative agencies" of State government? While the Cabinet officers are called "administrative officers" by the Constitution, the term "administrative agencies" usually is regarded nowadays as meaning the boards and bureaus set up for the regulation of business and industry and for the licensing and policing of professions, occupations, and trades. The typical administrative agency combines something of the executive, legislative, and judicial functions. The Hotel and Restaurant Commissioner can, for example, make a regulation (legislative), enforce this regulation (executive), and impose a fine for its violation (judicial). The Commissioner can do all these things only because the Legislature has clothed him with this authority, and the courts are always open to anyone who accuses the Commissioner of going beyond his lawful authority.

Q.—Can I report poor service in a hotel to the Florida Hotel and Restaurant Commission, and what good would it do?
The answer to the first part of your question is definitely yes.

The answer to the second part depends on several factors. If the poor service is the result of substandard equipment or conditions, the Hotel and Restaurant Commission has the jurisdiction and authority to require improvements and compliance with laws of safety and sanitation. If it is the result of a management problem, the Commission is in a position to conduct a review of the operations by a field representative of the Hospitality Education Program (HEP), who is an expert in the lodging field and who will recommend a solution. (This HEP program was started by the Commission, is financially sustained from the Commission's budget, and is administered by the Florida State University.) If the poor service is the result of a lack of trained and competent personnel, the manager can again be advised by HEP personnel that courses are available for training in vocational skills in many of our vocational and technical schools, supervisory training in some of our junior colleges, and management education at the Florida State University.

If the poor service is the result of the factors outside the jurisdiction of the Commission, the manager is advised of the complaint and encouraged to correct the deficiency. It is pointed out that he is not properly serving the public by not fulfilling his objective of providing clean and comfortable accommodations with courteous service, and is thereby damaging his own business and casting a shadow on Florida's Hospitality Industry. [Hotel and Restaurant Commissioner]

Q.—People speak of the "Hotel and Restaurant Commission" and the "Hotel and Restaurant Commissioner." Which is correct?
There is no Hotel and Restaurant Commission in the sense of a board. The Commission is the agency. The Commissioner is the officer. The Commissioner is responsible to no one, except in the general way that every non-Cabinet officer of the Executive Department is accountable to the Governor and the courts for specific misdoing. The same is true of the Motor Vehicle Commission. There is no "commission," and never has been. The Motor Vehicle Commissioner is the sole responsible officer.

Q.—How many kinds of State boards and commissions are there?
This must be a matter of opinion. Even so, all boards cannot be pressed into firm categories for there are overlappages of function. It could be said there are boards on *admissions*. These have as their primary function the examining of applicants for the professions: among them architects, lawyers, and doctors. But these boards also exercise some regulatory power through the ability to withdraw the right of a person to practice because, perhaps, of conviction of some criminal act. Then there are *regulatory* boards. An example is the Public Utilities Commission, which has the duty of protecting the public interest as to rates and service. There are *administrative* boards. The Board of Commissioners of State Institutions administers (among other public installations) the prisons and mental health hospitals. There are *advisory* boards. The Governor's Mansion Commission makes recommendations for the maintenance and upkeep of the State's residence for its first family. The Bond Review Committee is an example of a board with a dual purpose. It has the responsibility for approving (or disapproving) the issuance of certain State securities. But it also is charged with making recommendations to the Legislature on fiscal affairs. Finally, there are *temporary* boards. The Council on Economic Development was created by a governor for the purpose of determining if and how the State govern-

ment should assemble information of a statistical nature. Once this mission was finished, COED passed out of existence.

Q.—Can citizens complain to the State regulatory boards?
Yes. For example, the three regulatory boards administered through the office of the Secretary of State are the Labor Business Agents, Private Employment Agencies, and Private Investigative Agencies. Any person who has a grievance against a labor business agent, private employment agency, or private investigative agency, which had been licensed through the Secretary of State, upon complaint to the Secretary of State would receive a formal accusation form to be executed, notarized, and returned to this office. At that time a field agent from this office would investigate the charges, and if there appeared to be cause to suspend or revoke the license of the agency, a letter would be sent to the licensee stating the complaint and setting a 30-day notice for a public hearing. After this public hearing, usually heard by a deputy commissioner, or a representative from this office, an order would be issued either recommending, or not recommending, revocation of the agency's license. If the licensee were dissatisfied with the recommendation, he would have recourse to appeal the issue to the courts. [Secretary of State]

Q.—Does the State Purchasing Commission do all the buying for the State agencies?
The Purchasing Commission does not purchase for all State agencies. It has absorbed all purchasing functions previously under the Board of Commissioners of State Institutions. This embraces the actual purchases of the requirements of the Board's 19 institutions. In addition to this function, the Commission handles and approves the purchase of all types of automotive equipment such as passenger vehicles, trucks, draglines, bulldozers, including boats, aircraft, and other heavy equipment. Further, all State agencies are subject to the statutory and regulatory authority of the Purchasing Commission. [Director, Purchasing Commission]

Q.—What does the Inspection Division of the Department of Agriculture do?
The Inspection Division, headquartered in the Nathan Mayo Building in Tallahassee, has the responsibility of enforcing various regulatory laws administered by the Department of Agriculture.
Inspectors of this Division have the responsibility for enforcing

the Commercial Feed Law, Commercial Fertilizer Law, Pesticide Law, Seed Law, and the Seed Certification Law; and in addition they help to enforce the Egg Law, Poultry Law, Weights and Measures Law, and the Food, Drug, and Cosmetic Law.

The Division also has the duty of operating road-guard inspection stations and of performing the general inspection activities relating to the movement of agricultural, horticultural, and livestock products and commodities.

All records pertaining to the enforcement of the above-mentioned laws are kept by the Inspection Division, and samples of products coming under these laws are collected at frequent intervals by the inspectors and are sent to the State Chemist for analysis.

Most of the above laws also require the registration of the manufacturer's products and correct labeling of weight and ingredients. Inspections are made frequently to see that manufacturers comply with the standard of the law. [Commissioner of Agriculture]

Q.—If I support a candidate for Governor with money and time, can I get a job in his administration?

Like so many questions in politics, the answer to this must be "It depends." It depends upon what you have in mind as "a job." If you mean employment, part of the answer will be the availability of a job for which you can qualify. Most of the jobs in the agencies under the Governor are filled nowadays from eligibility lists established by the merit system after examinations. As a political friend, you may be given preference when a job becomes available, but you must be among the top five on the eligible list. The merit system discourages dismissals among government workers, so the turnover is about the same as it would be in any comparable private office. If by "a job" you mean an appointment by the Governor to an office or commission, the question of eligibility again arises. The Governor makes about 3,000 appointments during his four-year term. Most of these are to local boards: library boards, mosquito control boards, hospital boards, and the like. To be eligible for these (and by far the majority carry only the compensation of public service), you must live in the county or district. The Governor also makes many appointments to professional licensing and examining boards. There again, the persons to be considered for appointment must be members of the particular board's profession. Still other appointments are made to paying public offices when incumbents die, retire, or resign. Gen-

erally, Governors prefer to appoint people to these offices who intend
to run for election. So the overall answer must be "It depends."

Q.—How many State employees are there?
The number of State employees varies from month to month. This
variation results from the seasonal nature of some occupations: the
inspection of citrus fruit, for example. However, there are usually
around 45,000 persons on the State government's payroll. The Road
Department is the largest departmental employer, followed by the
University of Florida and the Florida State University.

Q.—Does Florida have a State civil service?
The 1955 Florida Legislature created a Merit System of Personnel
Administration covering the employees of the federal grant-in-aid
agencies and "employees of such other state agencies as the Governor,
other constitutional officers, or the Railroad and Public Utilities
Commission may direct . . ." (Chapter 110, Florida Statutes). The
function of a merit system is essentially the same as a civil service
system. In addition to the grant-in-aid agencies, which are the Civil
Defense Agency, Crippled Children's Commission, State Board of
Health, Industrial Commission, Department of Public Welfare, the
Hospital Construction Section of the Development Commission, and
the Merit System agency itself, the following agencies under the
jurisdiction of the Governor have been placed under the system:
Auditing Department, Barbers Sanitary Commission, Beverage De-
partment, the Salt Water Conservation and the Geological Survey
Departments of the Board of Conservation, Development Commis-
sion, Hotel and Restaurant Commission, Motor Vehicle Commission,
Board of Parks and Historic Memorials, Racing Commission, and
State Road Department. At the present time, approximately 15,000
State employees are covered by the Florida Merit System, which
represents approximately one-third of the total number of State
employees. [Director, Merit System Council]

Q.—What is the "classified service" of the Merit System?
The classified service constitutes the positions in public employment
which have Merit System coverage. They are "classified" by uniform
job description and pay categories.

Q.—Can State employees engage in politics?
Section 110.13 of the Merit System Law prohibits employees in the

classified service from making contributions to, or soliciting for, political organizations. In addition, no Merit System employee may be a candidate for nomination or election to any paid public office or take any part in the management or affairs of any political party or in any political campaign, except to exercise his right as a citizen privately to express his opinion and to cast his vote. According to the law, persons who willfully violate the provisions of this section are subject to such disciplinary action as may be prescribed by the State Personnel Board (the Cabinet). [Director, Merit System Council]

Q.—What is the State militia?
In a section of the Constitution reminiscent of frontier days, the State militia is declared to be composed of "all able bodied male inhabitants of the State between the ages of eighteen and forty-five years, that are citizens of the United States, or have declared their intention to become citizens thereof. . . ." There also is a statute in generally the same words.

Q.—Is there a force known as the State militia in being now?
Florida's militia consists of "organized military forces," such as the National Guard and the State Guard, and the "unorganized," those "able-bodied male citizens" between the ages of eighteen and forty-five who are, by Constitution and law, liable to be called to duty. In the event the Florida National Guard is ordered into the federal forces, the law provides for the recruitment of the Florida State Guard. The State Guard serves the needs of the State government during the period until the National Guard is restored to State control.

Q.—Does the Governor possess the exclusive power to call out the Florida National Guard when the Guard is in State service?
The Governor is the commander in chief of the Florida National Guard and other State military forces. (Interestingly, the law says "he shall not command personally in the field unless advised to do so by a resolution of the Legislature.") In the event there are disturbances civil authorities are unable to quell, and the Governor cannot be reached in time, the Adjutant General may call out the necessary number of troops. The law, in reciting the Governor's powers to deploy the National Guard, refers also to another "person lawfully administering the government of the State," but without further describing this individual. This would appear to mean that

in an emergency, with the Governor absent or incapacitated, some officer of the State in addition to the Adjutant General also might mobilize the troops to preserve life and property.

Q.—How do you write to the Governor?
The Governor may be addressed as "The Honorable John Doe, Governor, Tallahassee, Florida, Dear Governor Doe," or as "The Governor, Tallahassee, Florida, Dear Governor Doe."

Q.—How much money does the Governor make (including allowances)?
The Governor's annual cash salary is $25,000. The Governor's Mansion is his residence, for which there is an annual operating appropriation of $36,450. He is furnished a State car and a Highway Patrol lieutenant as an aide and driver. [Director, Budget Commission]

Q.—Is it required by law that the Governor hold press conferences?
No. This is entirely a matter of gubernatorial discretion. Press conferences on a regular weekly basis were commenced at Tallahassee during the administration of Governor LeRoy Collins in the 1950's. There had been occasional press conferences, particularly during legislative sessions, during prior administrations. It is unlikely that they will ever be discontinued because the conferences serve as an excellent forum for getting the Governor's views to the people without the formality which was attached to the prepared statements of prior years. The informality of the press conference allows considerable helpful leeway for both the Governor and the correspondents. Transcripts of the press conferences are sent by the Governor to newspapers, television and radio stations, and to others who might be interested in the text of what was said.

Q.—How many people does a Governor appoint to public office?
A Governor will have the opportunity of making approximately 3,000 appointments during a four-year term. It should be remembered that by far the majority of these public offices are of a local nature: county hospital boards, library boards, jury commissions, drainage control boards, and the like. It also should be kept in mind that most of these positions are honorary, in the sense that they carry no pay beyond the reward of being able to serve the community. The Governor will fill vacancies in State and county elective offices

which occur during the terms of those officers by reason of death, resignation, or removal. Exceptions: The Governor cannot make appointments to the State Legislature or to the United States House of Representatives. Vacancies in these offices can be filled only by the voters. When desirable, the Governor can call special elections for this purpose.

Q.—Can visitors tour the Governor's Mansion?
Yes. It is helpful to make an advance request so that conflicts with official functions and resident affairs can be avoided. [Office of the Governor]

Q.—What happens if the Governor dies in office?
If the Governor dies, he is succeeded by the President of the Senate, who serves as Governor either for the remainder of the term or, if a general election intervenes, until a new Governor can be elected and inaugurated. If there is no President of the Senate, because of death, expiration of his term, or some other reason, the Speaker of the House of Representatives succeeds to the office of Governor.

Q.—Can a Governor resign?
Yes. Section 19 of Article IV of the Constitution includes "resignation" among the circumstances which would cause the President of the Senate to succeed the Governor. No elected Governor has resigned.

Q.—What happens if a Governor becomes incapacitated?
That's a question which, in turn, presents a number of legal questions that have never been answered in Florida. The Constitution provides for the President of the Senate to succeed in the event of the "inability" of a Governor to "discharge his official duties." The Constitution also says the Governor can reclaim his office when "the disability shall cease." However, no way is provided for a determination either of the "inability" or the cessation of the "disability" other than by the Governor himself. During the long illness of Governor Fred P. Cone in the 1930's, study was made of this question and thought was given to the preparation of a lawsuit to seek an answer. This was abandoned after Governor Cone, in a Jacksonville hospital, made himself accessible to enough people to demonstrate his capacity for discharging his duties.

Q.—Who was the youngest Governor of Florida?
Through the inauguration of Farris Bryant as Governor in January,

1961, the youngest elected Governor was Park Trammell of Lakeland. At the moment of his inauguration in 1913, Governor Trammell (afterwards United States Senator) was thirty-six. The average age of Florida governors at the time of taking the oath of office, ranging from Governor Fred P. Cone's sixty-five years to Governor Trammell's thirty-six, was 48.6 years.

Q.—If I have a complaint about telephone service, to what public agency could I address my complaint?
To the Public Utilities Commission at Tallahassee.

Q.—What else does the Public Utilities Commission regulate?
This agency, known until lately as the Railroad and Public Utilities Commission, has the duty of making "reasonable and just" rates and overseeing the service of transportation companies, telephone and telegraph companies, privately owned electric and gas companies, and privately owned water and sewer companies.

Q.—Is the Florida Public Utilities Commission like such federal regulatory agencies as the Federal Trade Commission and the Civil Aeronautics Board?
There are similarities, mainly in that the Public Utilities Commission combines judicial, legislative, and executive functions. The Public Utilities Commission is different in that its three members are elected. The members of the federal agencies, like those of State boards generally, are appointed.

Q.—Who is eligible to run for membership on the Public Utilities Commission?
Any person qualified to vote is eligible to be elected to the Public Utilities Commission.

Q.—Are the members of the Public Utilities Commission elected by districts or statewide? For what term?
The three members of the PUC are elected statewide, for four-year terms. This means that two members are elected regularly in one election, and another in the next election two years later.

Q.—How many professions or trades are regulated by State boards?
There are at least twenty-nine professions or trades regulated by State boards, and a reasonable case could be stated for inclusion of several more. In these, a State agency has the right to revoke or refuse to issue an occupational license. This could be regarded as

regulation even in the absence of the companion power to test qualifications.

Q.—What are the regulated professions or trades?
Certified public accountants, architects, lawyers, barbers, cosmetologists, chiropodists, chiropractors, dentists, engineers, pest exterminators, foresters, funeral directors and embalmers, labor business agents, masseurs, medical doctors, physical therapists, naturopaths, nurses, dispensing opticians, optometrists, osteopaths, pharmacists, pilot commissioners, psychologists, real estate brokers and salesmen, sanitarians, teachers, veterinarians, and watchmakers.

Q.—How are the members of these boards chosen?
Generally, the members are appointed by the Governor from among Florida practitioners of the particular profession or trade.

Q.—Are there any other "product" commissions besides the Citrus Commission and the Egg Commission?
None other so specifically established. It could be contended that the Conservation Department serves this purpose with its intensive program for popularizing "lisa," or Florida mullet. Both the Department of Agriculture and the Development Commission promote the use of Florida agricultural and industrial products. And the Racing Commission administers funds set aside by the Legislature to encourage horsebreeding in Florida by providing special purses for home-state races. The Milk Commission is concerned mainly with price-fixing.

Q.—Where are State office buildings besides in Tallahassee?
There are "branch capitols" in Tampa, Miami, and Winter Park, making possible the grouping of State public service offices in those areas. Agencies of the State government, notably the Industrial Commission, the Department of Public Safety (Highway Patrol), the Road Department, and the Military Department, own numerous buildings for their own occupancy.

Q.—Does the Crippled Children's Commission help children who are not crippled?
The word "crippled" has a professional meaning that goes beyond orthopedic, or bone, ailments. A "crippled child" is defined for this purpose as any boy or girl of less than twenty-one years whose "physical functions or movements are impaired by accident, disease, or congenital deformity" and those suffering from any disease or condition which is likely to result in a crippling condition.

Q.—Does the Crippled Children's Commission run hospitals?
No. The Commission provides professional care in approved hospitals, clinics, and other medical centers for physically impaired children.

Q.—Who writes the advertisements for the State of Florida that appear in national newspapers and magazines?
These are prepared by private advertising agencies which have been retained by the Florida Development Commission. The Commission and its staff will pass upon the general policy line of a particular advertising program (the appeal, say, for summer visitors), and then upon the specific advertisements proposed to be used in this series.

Q.—What else does the Development Commission do?
The Development Commission holds an extremely broad mandate from the Legislature for the promotion of the general well-being of the State. In part, the law says the Commission shall "guide, stimulate, and promote the coordinated, efficient, and beneficial development" of the state and its regions. Tourist promotion is one face of its labors. Industrial development is another. The agency also finances revenue bond programs, serves as the middleman for getting surplus federal products into local hands, and works with the federal government in programs relating to hospitals, aviation, and other purposes.

Q.—Does the State Auditor check the books of all State agencies?
The State Auditor is required by law to make an annual audit of the accounts and records of all State and county offices, including boards and institutions.

Q.—Does the Governor have the sole right to refuse extradition?
The Governor is the Chief Executive of the State; in issuing the warrant of extradition he acts under the authority of his sovereign State and he may, on its behalf, refuse to grant extradition. Even if the refusal is on grounds not legally warranted, it seems there is no power delegated to the federal government, either through the judiciary or otherwise, to use any coercive means to compel him to grant extradition. [Office of the Governor]

Q.—Can I will my body to the medical school?
The Anatomical Board of Florida is specifically authorized to accept bodies willed for the advancement of medical science. This board

represents all the medical schools in the state. It disposes primarily of unclaimed bodies and those of the pauper dead.

Q.—How does the Citrus Commission set minimum standards for fruit?

The Florida Citrus Commission has promulgated a number of regulations establishing minimum maturity and quality standards for citrus fruit. These regulations implement minimum maturity standards which are established by State law for most varieties. In addition, the Commission, by regulation, prescribes the methods to be used to test for maturity and to determine quality. Before promulgating these regulations, the Commission seeks the advice and recommendations of the various industry groups, including grower organizations, fresh-fruit shippers, canners, and Department of Agriculture officials. [General Manager, Citrus Commission]

Q.—Is the Citrus Commission financed entirely by the Citrus industry?

Yes. At the request of the Florida citrus industry, the State Legislature enacted legislation to create the Florida Citrus Commission and at the same time levied an excise tax on all citrus fruit produced in Florida to defray the costs of operation of the Commission. [General Manager, Citrus Commission]

Q.—What is the difference between a state bank and a national bank?

A national bank is chartered under federal law and supervised by the Comptroller of the Currency, Washington, D. C. A state bank is chartered by state law and in Florida is supervised by the Comptroller, ex-officio State Commissioner of Banking.

There are other differences but none apparent to the typical depositor. Federal examiners supervise national banks; state examiners oversee state banks, for example. National banks keep their reserves in one place, state banks in another. In Florida, all national banks and all state banks but one have deposits up to $10,000 insured by the Federal Deposit Insurance Corporation.

The Legislature, the Laws, and the Lobbyists

Q.—When does the Legislature meet?

Regularly, the Legislature meets on the first Tuesday after the first Monday in April of odd-numbered years. This regular session lasts sixty consecutive days (Sundays included). The Governor and the Legislature may call special sessions.

Q.—How does the Legislature call itself into session?

The "self-starter" amendment of 1956 to the Constitution allows the Legislature to convene itself in a session limited to thirty days. This can be brought about if 20 per cent of the members of the Legislature file with the Secretary of State certificates stating conditions warrant the convening of the extra session. The Secretary of State then, within seven days, shall poll all the members of the Legislature. If he receives an affirmative vote from three-fifths of the legislators, the Secretary of State then shall fix the day and hour for convening the session. Up to 1964, the "self-starter" had not been used.

Q.—Can the Legislature, independently of the Governor, continue in session after the expiration of the sixty days of the regular session?

Yes. This has been possible since the Constitution was amended in 1954 to permit extended sessions. A regular session may be extended by the vote of three-fifths of the membership of both houses. The extension may be for a total of thirty days, but these need not be consecutive days. (The sixty days of a regular session are consecutive days, including Sundays.) But the thirty non-consecutive days may not carry the Legislature beyond September 1 after the regular session. This provision has been used by the Legislature several times to complete its business.

Q.—How do I write to a member of the Legislature?

During sessions of the Legislature a person may write to a member at the State Capitol, Tallahassee. Between sessions one should write to the member's home address. Members' names and addresses are published in a number of places or can be obtained from local public officials. If other means fail, this information can always be obtained from the Secretary of State, Tallahassee. When writing a member, one should know as much about his subject as possible and be as specific as possible in expressing his view. [Director, Legislative Reference Bureau]

Q.—How can a citizen get a bill introduced in the Legislature?

Bills can be introduced in the Legislature only by members. Therefore, a citizen who wants a bill introduced must find a Senator or Representative who is willing to introduce it for him. [Director, Legislative Reference Bureau]

Q.—Do legislators write their own bills?

Generally, no. The largest number of bills drawn in any one place are prepared in the Bill Drafting Division of the Office of the Attorney General, which was created to furnish this service. This Division also circulates information on the technicalities of bill drafting to city attorneys, county attorneys, and others who might be called upon to perform this task.

Q.—Is it possible for a layman to understand the parliamentary procedure in the Legislature?

Yes, in the same sense that the layman can understand the rules of a football game or the ritual of a fraternal order: by seeking out the reasons why procedure takes the course that it does. Some of the most successful members of the Legislature have been non-lawyers. Parliamentary procedure is a time-tested way of achieving results in a situation which brings together a large group of people of diverse backgrounds, experiences, and purposes for a relatively short period of time. The House of Representatives publishes a guide to its proceedings which is helpful to visitors.

Q.—What is meant by "introduction and reference" of bills?

Bills may be introduced only by a member of the Legislature. A Senator or Representative with a bill to introduce will send it to the office of the Senate Secretary or the House Chief Clerk. There it will be numbered and formally "introduced" by having its title read to the Senate or House when opportunity occurs in the daily order of business. A bill is "referred" by the Senate President, House Speaker, or by the house itself, to an appropriate committee (or committees). While the presiding officers possess considerable discretion in the reference of bills to committees, this is not absolute. For example, all bills making an appropriation of State money must go to the Committee on Appropriations.

Q.—How many bills are introduced each session? How many are passed?

In most of the recent sessions there have been nearly 4,000 bills introduced each session. In these sessions, there have been about 2,000 general bills, of which a little over a quarter—between 500 and 600—were enacted into law. In these sessions there usually are just under 2,000 bills of local or limited application, and most of these are passed.

	1963	
	Introduced	Passed
General Bills	2,013	572
Local, Limited, and Miscellaneous Bills and Resolutions	1,951	1,475
Total	3,964	2,047

[Director, Legislative Reference Bureau]

Q.—How many State laws are there?

Florida in 1964 had 7,543 general laws, plus 33,099 local laws. The local laws applied to one or more counties or cities. Many of the laws are considered obsolete but are still on the books. About 3,000 of the general laws and 15,000 of the local laws are regarded as being in the "active" category. The Legislature adds some 1,700 new laws every two years. The oldest, unrevised law enacted in Florida was passed in 1822 and authorizes a notary to administer oaths. Florida is, however, a common-law state, which means that laws of England existing prior to July 4, 1776, are still in force in Florida unless specifically repealed or superseded.

Q.—Are all the laws of Florida published in one book?

No, it requires several books just to publish the laws enacted by a single regular session of the Legislature. The continuing body of laws applying statewide, known as *Florida Statutes,* is published in three volumes.

Q.—What subject produces the greatest volume of proposed general legislation, from session to session?

Education, first; then, in order, taxation, motor vehicles, criminal law, courts, elections, and conservation of natural resources. [Director, Statutory Revision, Office of the Attorney General]

Q.—With so many laws in force, are there many conflicts?

Very few, because Florida has a continuous revision system which brings about the revising, repealing, and amending of standing laws every two years and the publication of an up-to-date edition of the statutory (general) laws shortly after every regular session of the Legislature. [Director, Statutory Revision, Office of the Attorney General]

Q.—Does the Governor have to approve every bill passed by the Legislature?

No, he has the right to veto every legislative act (a "bill" becomes an "act" after passage by the Legislature). A vetoed act can become law only if repassed by two-thirds of the members present in each house. During a legislative session, the Governor has five days (not including Sundays) to decide whether he will (1) sign the act into law, (2) allow it to become law automatically without his signature at the expiration of the five days, or (3) veto it. If the session of the Legislature ends before the Governor has had the five-day opportunity to consider what course he will take, he then has twenty days. Because a great amount of legislation, and particularly acts of considerable importance, reach the Governor after the lawmakers have gone home, his veto then has the result of holding the measure in suspense until the next session. Often, this delay amounts to killing the measure. On the specific question of whether the Governor has "to approve every bill," the technical reply could be that numerically more acts become law without his approval than do otherwise. This is by reason of the fact that most Governors allow local bills to become law without their approving signature.

Q.—How important is the veto power of the Governor?

More so than it seems, for the legislative machinery is geared so that most acts reach the Governor during the period when he can wait until the legislators have gone home before announcing his vetoes. The practical result of this time lag is that the Governor's wishes usually prevail, at least for the two years before the Legislature returns for the next regular session.

What should be kept in mind is that acts usually take a week or more after passage to go through the process of enrollment (copying on special paper for permanent record) and signature by the presiding officers and clerks of the two legislative houses. Infrequently, an act may be of such significance that it will be rushed through this process. But generally the deluge of legislative business washes up in the Governor's office after the calendar has run out on the five-day period.

The Governor possesses a special veto power in the consideration of acts making more than one appropriation. He can go into these to strike out an item or items, leaving stand those he approves. This is a power which the President of the United States lacks. The President may reluctantly accept part of an appropriations measure in order to have another part he wants to become law.

Q.—What is the difference between a "statute" and a "law"?
They are synonymous in that both connote a rule of organized society. A statute indicates, more specifically, a legislative enactment; the statutory law as distinguished from the common law. The common law is that made by courts in deciding cases. [Judge Wallace E. Sturgis, First District Court of Appeal]

Q.—Is there always a ceremony when the Governor signs a bill?
No, but legislators or others interested in a particular measure may ask to be notified in advance of the time that the Governor expects to sign an act. This will enable them to arrange for a photographer to capture the scene so they may have a memento of the occasion. Typically, this "ceremony" will take less than five minutes, given largely to the photographer's grouping of the people to be in the picture.

Q.—Are the terms "bill" and "act" used interchangeably?
Technically, as already explained, a bill becomes an act during the period between passage by the Legislature and, assuming no veto by the Governor, its effective date as a law. Actually, that change in its status is seldom recognized in writing or talking about a bill. The title of every bill does, however, serve to remind of the difference, for all these read "A Bill to be Entitled An Act. . . ."

Q.—Do all laws become effective on the same date?
The Constitution says "no law shall take effect until sixty days from the final adjournment of the session of the Legislature at which it

may have been enacted, unless otherwise specially provided in such law." This delay was intended to give the public an opportunity to learn of new laws. While the Office of the Secretary of State has tried to encourage the use of this uniform date, so there would be time for the printing and distribution of the text of new laws, many laws become operative in shorter time. An effective clause often found in bills reads: "This law shall become effective upon becoming a law"—in a word, immediately.

Q.—Are many bills which pass the Legislature and become law then "thrown out" by the Supreme Court?
Perhaps one or two from each regular session. Actually, considering the large number passed, remarkably few are challenged.

Q.—What is a local bill?
A local bill is one which affects only a specific locality, such as a city or county. The Constitution requires that notice of a local bill be published in the locality prior to the bill's introduction, or that the bill be subject to a referendum vote in the locality before it becomes effective. The Constitution also prohibits local bills on certain subjects. [Director, Legislative Reference Bureau]

Q.—What are those "certain subjects"?
The Legislature cannot lawfully pass special or local laws (Article III, Section 20) making exceptions to laws of statewide application relating to (among other categories) the administration of justice, the assessment and collection of taxes, the conducting of elections, the property and rights of children, the granting of divorces, the changing of names of persons, the recognition of informal or invalid deeds and wills, and the establishment of ferries.

Q.—Who can run for the Legislature?
Anyone can run for the Legislature who is an elector in the county or district which he seeks to serve. Basically, an elector is any person twenty-one or over who, at the time of registration to vote, is a citizen of the United States and has been a permanent resident of Florida for one year and of his county for six months. Specifically, no person holding "a lucrative office or appointment" in the State or federal government is eligible to serve in the Legislature, but "office" has been defined as a place for which the officer receives a commission signed either by the Governor or the President. In other words, so

prominent an "official" as the Director of the Board of Conservation is technically an "employee" and not an "officer."

Q.—How much does it cost to run for the Legislature?

The qualifying fee for candidates for Senator and Representative, as it is for candidates for other State offices, is 5 per cent of the salary for the first year. Thus, legislative aspirants pay $60. That is the legal cost of running for the Legislature. The actual cost of candidacy depends, of course, upon the campaign which a particular aspirant feels he needs to wage and, likely, the pocketbooks of the candidate and his backers.

Q.—How much pay do legislators get?

Legislators are paid $100 a month.

Q.—Do legislators get expense accounts?

Yes, in the sense of being paid a daily allowance for expenses during sessions. The amount of this allowance has been changed by the Legislature from time to time but the 1963 session authorized the payment of $25 a day. Additionally, legislators are paid the equivalent of one round trip, at the rate of 10 cents a mile, between their place of residence and Tallahassee for each week of a session. Legislators also receive secretarial help, local telephone service, and a postage allowance during regular sessions. Legislative service is applied on the years required for participation in the State retirement system.

Q.—Can I get a job during legislative sessions?

That depends upon several factors, including your degree of competence and the number of applicants. Usually, there are considerably more applicants than jobs. The members of the Legislature select their own "attachés," as legislative workers are known. Others are employed by the Senate Secretary and Sergeant-at-Arms and the House Chief Clerk and Sergeant-at-Arms, and the chairmen of the personnel committees in the two houses.

Q.—What is an attaché?

This word, originally French with the accent on the third syllable, *shay,* has a special legislative meaning. All employees of the Legislature, regardless of rank, are known as attachés. The word suggests the personal nature of legislative employment, with Senators and Representatives entitled as a matter of privilege to have a specified number of persons put on the payroll.

Q.—What is a page in the Legislature?

These are the youngsters, usually from ten to sixteen years of age and often children of legislators, who carry messages and do other errands for Senators and Representatives in the chambers during sessions. (The heavier, more responsible tasks are performed by assistants to the Sergeants-at-Arms.) The experience affords an opportunity for involvement in the lawmaking process which, depending upon the interest of the child, could be both fascinating and helpful.

Q.—Does the Legislature publish a calendar?

Each morning each house publishes a calendar for that day's considerations. [Director, Legislative Reference Bureau]

Q.—Does the Legislature publish a daily record like the Congressional Record?

The Senate and the House of Representatives each publishes a daily journal of the actions it takes. Unlike the Congressional Record, these journals do not contain the remarks of members. However, in accordance with a requirement of the Florida Constitution, they contain the vote of the members on final passage of every bill. [Director, Legislative Reference Bureau]

Q.—Can anyone watch the Legislature in session?

Yes, public galleries are provided in both the Senate and the House of Representatives. An exception: the Senate has occasional "executive" sessions, with the chamber and galleries cleared of everyone except Senators and the Senate's Secretary. Primarily, these sessions are for the consideration of appointments made by the Governor to offices requiring Senate confirmation.

Q.—Are Democrats and Republicans separated in the Legislature as they are in Congress?

No distinction in seating is made between the Democratic and Republican members of the Legislature. In the House, seating is by counties and all Representatives from a particular county are seated together. In the Senate, numerical designation of a district controls almost generally the location of a Senator's desk. There are exceptions but these have nothing to do with party affiliation.

Q.—How long has the Legislature been meeting in Tallahassee?

The Legislative Council, predecessor of the Legislature, had its first meeting in Tallahassee, the new capital, on November 8, 1824.

Q.—How does the Senate vote?
The Senate votes by voice, each Senator giving his aye or nay vote as the roll is called. [Director, Legislative Reference Bureau]

Q.—How does the House vote?
The House Chamber is equipped with an electric vote-tally machine. On each member's desk there is a switch which he may press one way to vote aye and the other to vote nay. His vote is shown on a large name board at the front of the Chamber. When all members have voted, the machine automatically adds the aye and nay votes and posts the totals at the top of the name board. It also punches onto a paper record the vote of each member and the totals. [Director, Legislative Reference Bureau]

Q.—What is a special session of the Legislature and why are special sessions called?
A special session of the Legislature is one other than the regular sixty-day, every-other-year session provided by the Constitution. Special sessions of various types may be called either by the Governor or by the Legislature. They can be called for any reason that seems appropriate, such as unfinished business of the regular legislative session, need for new revenue, or a try at legislative apportionment.

Q.—Does the Legislature need to meet so often?
Legislative reapportionment and taxation for the financing of State government have been the reasons for an unusual number of special sessions in recent years. Whether the necessity for more frequent special sessions will continue remains to be seen. There are those who feel the Legislature no longer can conduct the State's business in sixty-day biennial sessions. Legislative committees have studied a number of alternatives, including annual sessions, but the voters have yet to pass on any of these proposals.

Q.—What hours does the Legislature keep?
If hours in actual daily session is meant, this depends upon the stage of the proceeding. During the first thirty days, or more, of the regular sixty-day session, the Legislature customarily meets for a few hours a day, with the rest of the day given over to committees for meetings on the mass of legislation which has been proposed. Gradually, as the committees progress with their work, more time becomes available for Chamber action upon the bills which have cleared. Certainly during the last twenty days both houses will be meeting morning and after-

noon. This means that the committees may begin meeting then at 7:00 A.M., suspend during sessions in the chambers, and resume afterwards to continue into the evening.

Q.—Can anyone become a lobbyist?

Any person may become a lobbyist. The requirements he must meet in order to lobby are contained in Sections 11.05 and 11.06, Florida Statutes, and in the Rules of the House of Representatives. [Director, Legislative Reference Bureau]

Q.—How many lobbyists attend a session of the Legislature?

Only the House of Representatives requires the registration of persons who appear before its committees. During the 1963 regular session, 653 persons registered, and these appeared on behalf of 546 interests —an "interest" ranges from an individual expressing his personal approval or disapproval of some measure to organizations and governmental agencies. [Chief Clerk, House of Representatives]

Q.—When and where do committees of the Legislature meet?

During a legislative session, committees meet at posted times and in assigned rooms. In the House, the Speaker groups committees so that they can meet at regular days and hours. Senate committees make their own determination of when and where to meet.

Q.—Can anyone attend a legislative committee meeting?

Yes, although there are times when a committee will try to exclude the public. Conference committees are a special situation, as they customarily meet privately. These are committees composed of members of the Senate and the House, who are appointed for the purpose of seeking to settle the differences between the two legislative bodies on a particular bill.

Q.—Has there ever been a member of the Legislature who was a member of a third party?

Along with Democrats and Republicans, there have been Socialist, Populist, and Whig members of the Florida Legislature.

Q.—Can anyone get on the mailing list for the House and Senate Journals?

A request to your Senator and Representative should suffice.

Q.—What is the Legislative Council?

The Legislative Council is a joint permanent interior committee of legislators representing all sections of the state who supervise research activities of the Reference Bureau and conduct studies of legislative problems between sessions of the Legislature. [Director, Legislative Reference Bureau]

Q.—What is the Legislative Reference Bureau?
The Reference Bureau is a staff of specially trained employees who furnish research information to the members of the Legislature and its committees. [Director, Legislative Reference Bureau]

Q.—Can anyone ask the Legislative Reference Bureau a question for research?
No, only members of the Legislature can.

Q.—Is there a problem of getting a quorum in the Legislature?
Generally, there is no problem about a quorum, which in the Senate and House of Representatives is defined as a majority of the members elected to each body. Because the work of lawmaking is concentrated in sixty consecutive days of a regular biennial session, nearly all members are almost always present. The exception has been an occasional Saturday session when the members have previously agreed not to consider controversial matters. Actually, the houses prefer to recess rather than meet on Saturdays because no agreement against considering controversial matters can cover all possibilities.

Q.—What is an impeachment?
Under Florida's Constitution, certain important public officers can be removed from office only by impeachment. These officers are the Governor and members of the Cabinet, the Justices of the Supreme Court, and the Judges of the District Courts of Appeal and of Circuit Courts. Impeachment is the process by which articles (charges) are voted by two-thirds of the members present of the House of Representatives. Trial follows in the Senate, and conviction occurs if two-thirds of the Senators present find the accused guilty.

Q.—How many impeachments have there been in Florida?
Articles of impeachment have been voted five times by the House of Representatives: against a Governor, a State Treasurer, and three Circuit Judges. Only two cases have been brought to trial in the Senate, and in neither of these (against Circuit Judges) was there a finding of guilt.

Q.—Can members of the Legislature be impeached?
No, but a Senator or Representative can be expelled by the agree-

ment of two-thirds of the members of his house. Expulsion could be regarded as more drastic than impeachment. Expulsion is final, the expelled legislator being without appeal. The executive or judicial officer impeached by the House must be tried by the Senate.

Q.—How can the State Constitution be amended?
The Legislature may propose amendments to the Constitution by a three-fifths vote of the members elected to each house. The amendment then is submitted to the statewide electorate for ratification or rejection. Only a majority of the persons actually voting upon the amendment need approve. The Constitution of 1885 had been amended 120 times by 1964.

Q.—Can the Governor veto a constitutional amendment?
No. He may be persuasive in seeking the adoption of an amendment by the Legislature and the electorate, but technically and actually he can do only what any other citizen may do—vote in the election.

Q.—Who sets the size of the congressional districts within a state?
The Legislature has this duty. When Congress has apportioned the number of districts among the states on the basis of the census, the legislatures must adjust the districts in those states where seats in the national House of Representatives have been gained or lost. Failure to re-district in that event means one or more seats will be on the statewide ballot at the next election for Congress. These seats are referred to as "at-large" seats, and the members elected to them are known as "Congressmen-at-large," since they represent the entire state rather than a single district.

Q.—Has Florida ever had a Congressman-at-large?
Since Florida first became entitled in 1874 to representation by more than one Congressman, there have been three "at-large" members, the most recent being R. A. (Lex) Green of Starke, in the 78th Congress (1943-1945).

Q.—Do legislative committees hold a hearing on every bill referred to them?
If by "hearing" you mean a formal call for persons to be heard in support of or opposition to "every" bill, the answer is "no." Generally, committees will hear from interested persons when bills are considered. Notice of the time and place of committee hearings is posted on bulletin boards in the lobbies of the two legislative houses. Not infrequently, however, a bill will be regarded as possessing such

interest that the committee will set a time of hearing far enough in advance for persons to come to Tallahassee for the purpose of appearing before the committee.

Q.—What is a conference committee?
A conference committee is established by the two houses when they have passed different versions of the same bill and it is felt that the points of disagreement can be adjusted. The versions will differ because, while using the same title, one house or the other has passed amendments to the bill. A conference committee is composed of equal numbers of Senators and Representatives. Conference committees meet privately. If the members of the conference committee have been able to agree upon a version, the two houses must vote upon this product. It still may be rejected.

Q.—Who may go on the floor of the House or Senate when the Legislature is in session?
Unless a special privilege is granted, only present members and designated employees of the Legislature, the Governor and Cabinet members, Justices of the Supreme Court, members of Congress, and former Governors, Cabinet members, or members of the Legislature may go upon the floor while a House is in session. [Director, Legislative Reference Bureau]

Q.—How are the Speaker of the House and the President of the Senate chosen?
The Senate President and House Speaker are elected by their fellow members. Actually, the members of the preceding session have designated the presiding officers for the current session. While it is true that some of the legislators participating in this designation will not be serving in the next session when the election actually will occur, there are advantages in choosing the presiding officers sufficiently in advance of the session so they may prepare themselves for this duty. Unlike those in many other states and the Congress of the United States, the Senate President and House Speaker in Florida do not serve successive sessions (and only rarely are re-elected after intervening sessions).

Q.—What is a joint session?
A joint session is the bringing together of the Senate and House of Representatives for the purpose of hearing the Governor "communicate . . . information concerning the condition of the State, and

recommend such measures as he may deem expedient" (Article IV, Section 9, Florida Constitution). The Legislature is convened in "joint meeting" to hear distinguished speakers. These usually include Florida's United States Senators. Although laymen use the terms "joint session" and "joint meeting" interchangeably, there is a technical difference.

Q.—Who was the first woman in the Legislature?
The first feminine member of the House was Mrs. Edna Giles Fuller of Orlando, who represented Orange County in the 1929 and 1931 Legislatures. The first woman to serve in the Florida Senate was Mrs. George W. (Beth) Johnson of Orlando, who was representing Orange County in the House when she was elected to a Senate vacancy in 1962. [Director, Legislative Reference Bureau]

Q.—What is a "pork chopper"?
It is a name applied to a group of Senators largely representing rural districts in the Florida Legislature. As originally used, the name referred to the majority bloc resisting reapportionment. Subsequently, a "pork chopper" might be a Senator who opposed some measure which the person using the term regarded as progressive. The opposing faction, or minority, in the reapportionment struggle was called "lamb-choppers," but this term never earned the popular acceptance enjoyed by the other label. There was the suggestion of the old Florida saying of "living high on the hog" in the "pork chop" appellation. It is related to the nationally accepted term of "pork barrel," or legislation which grants money from a federal or state treasury for local purposes. The tier of rural counties across North Florida, where many of the sparsely populated senatorial districts were found, also was known to some as the "hog and hominy (grits)" region, an alliterative reference to the staples of the farm table. "Pork Choppers" has its counterpart in the "Corn Stalk Brigade" and the "Black Horse Cavalry" of legislative blocs in other states.

Q.—Can the House and Senate Chambers be used for anything besides the Legislature?
Yes, especially when the Legislature is not in session, the Chambers are used for meetings of various nature: for the annual sessions of Boys' and Girls' States; for the opening and reading of bids on road contracts; and for other quasi-official gatherings of such size that cannot be accommodated in Capitol conference rooms.

The Courts, the Judges, and the Law Enforcers

Q.—How many different kinds of courts does Florida have?
There are fifteen constitutional and statutory courts, in addition to municipal courts and the Metropolitan courts of Dade County:
  (1) Appellate Courts:
    (a) The Supreme Court of Florida, and (b) three District Courts of Appeal.
  (2) Trial Courts:
    (a) Circuit Courts, (b) County Judge's Courts, (c) County Courts, (d) Criminal Courts of Record, (e) Civil Courts of Record (only one remaining—in Dade County), (f) Courts of Record, (g) Court of Record of Escambia County, (h) Civil and Criminal Court of Record (Pinellas County), (i) District County Court (Pinellas County), (j) Juvenile Courts, (k) Small Claims Courts, (l) Civil Claims Court (Hillsborough County), and (m) Justice of the Peace Courts. [Justice Stephen C. O'Connell, the Supreme Court]

Q.—How are judges selected in Florida?
Judges of all State courts are elected in the same manner as other public officials, except that Chapter 33, Florida Statutes, provides that Judges of Civil Courts of Record shall be appointed by the Governor and confirmed by the Senate. Municipal Judges are either appointed or elected in accordance with charter provisions which vary widely. Judges of the Metropolitan Court of Dade County are selected and elected under the "Missouri" or "American Bar Association" plan. In essence, this plan provides for an incumbent to be judged by the electorate on the basis of his record, rather than in a contest with another person. The question submitted to the voters is: "Shall Judge

Jones be retained in office?" Vacancies in all State courts are filled
through appointment by the Governor.

Q.—Does a judge have to be a lawyer?
Judges of the Supreme Court, the District Courts of Appeal, the Circuit Courts, the Court of Record of Escambia County, and the Criminal Courts of Record are required by the Constitution to be lawyers.

Judges of the Juvenile Courts, the Civil Courts of Record, and the
Small Claims Courts are required by general statute to be lawyers.

Judges of the other courts are not generally required to be lawyers,
though a special act of the Legislature may stipulate that a lawyer be
the judge of the court it creates. Many such acts do include the stipula-
tion. [Justice Stephen C. O'Connell, the Supreme Court]

Q.—What do Circuit Courts do?
To quote Article V, Section 6, of the Constitution of Florida: "The
circuit courts shall have exclusive original jurisdiction in all cases in
equity except such equity jurisdiction as may be conferred on juvenile
courts, in all cases at law not cognizable by subordinate courts, in all
cases involving the legality of any tax, assessment, or toll, in the action
of ejectment, in all actions involving the titles or boundaries of real
estate, and in all criminal cases not cognizable by subordinate courts.
They shall have original jurisdiction of actions of forcible entry and
unlawful detainer, and of such other matters as the legislature may
provide. They shall have final appellate jurisdiction in all civil and
criminal cases arising in the county court, or before county judges'
courts, of all misdemeanors tried in criminal courts of record, and
of all cases arising in municipal courts, small claims courts, and
courts of justices of the peace. The circuit courts and judges shall
have power to issue writs of mandamus, injunction, quo warranto,
certiorari, prohibition, and habeas corpus, and all writs necessary
or proper to the complete exercise of their jurisdiction."

The Circuit Courts' jurisdiction varies to some extent in the
different counties, because some of the larger counties have more
subordinate courts than others do, thereby relieving the Circuit
Courts in those counties of some of their jurisdiction. The Circuit
Court is the State's highest trial court, and it is also an appellate
court from subordinate courts, as stated in the above quotation from
the Constitution. In many counties, it is the trial court for all felonies
(criminal cases in which the penalty is death or imprisonment in the

state prison) and for all civil actions where the claim is over $100. It handles all chancery (equity) actions, such as injunction, divorce, and so forth. In counties which have Criminal Courts of Record, however, the Circuit Court's criminal jurisdiction is limited to capital cases—cases in which the maximum punishment is death. [Circuit Judge Guyte P. McCord, Jr.]

Q.—What is a Criminal Court of Record?
The Constitution authorizes the legislature to establish a Criminal Court of Record in any county.

These courts have power to try all criminal cases, less than capital, arising in the counties where they exist. They have no civil jurisdiction. The Circuit Court tries all capital cases. [Justice Stephen C. O'Connell, the Supreme Court]

Q.—What are District Courts of Appeal?
The Florida District Courts of Appeal, three in number, exercise appellate jurisdiction as provided by Article V, Section 5(3), Constitution of Florida. They handle the bulk of State appellate work.

Created in 1956 by constitutional amendment and activated in 1957, the District Courts of Appeal were designed to relieve the Florida Supreme Court of the intolerable burden of appellate work that had been cast upon it by reason of the great growth of Florida's population and economy, which has not abated; as a result, the work of the District Courts of Appeal has increased to the point where the Legislature has found it necessary to add two judges each in the Second and Third Districts and one in the First. There is a likelihood that additional districts will be required in the near future.

Except as otherwise provided by the state and federal constitutions, the decisions of the District Courts of Appeal are final in character.

These courts transact business in panels consisting of three judges. They sit to hear cases in any county where there is ready business to transact. [Chief Judge, First District Court of Appeal]

Q.—What kind of cases does a County Judge handle?
The County Judge generally has trial jurisdiction for misdemeanors and serves as committing magistrate in felony cases. He is responsible for the estates of deceased and incompetent persons. He is the judicial committing officer for mental institutions. He serves as coroner and investigates deaths of all persons who die under suspicious circumstances or without an attending physician. He is responsible for the

issuance of marriage licenses, drivers' licenses, and hunting and fishing licenses. The County Judge is the Chairman of the County Canvassing Board, which determines the official result of elections. He has concurrent jurisdiction with Small Claims Court Judges in some cases. He handles landlord-tenant, replevin, and attachment cases. [County Judge, Leon County]

Q.—What is a Small Claims Court?
A Small Claims Court, as the name indicates, is a statutory court having power to adjudicate only claims involving relatively small sums of money. Such courts exist in 42 counties and their jurisdiction varies from a low of $100 to a high of $1,000.

These courts are designed to expedite the settlement and collection of monetary claims under an inexpensive, simplified procedure which enables litigants to proceed without having to engage counsel to represent them. [Justice Stephen C. O'Connell, the Supreme Court]

Q.—How many counties in Florida still have Justice of the Peace Courts?
Forty counties had them in 1964. [Justice Stephen C. O'Connell, the Supreme Court]

Q.—How much do Circuit Judges make? Other judges?
Circuit Judges' compensation varies in the different circuits. The salary varies from $17,500 per year to $21,000 per year. Pay in subordinate courts varies in the different counties. Compensation of the Judges of the District Courts of Appeal is $18,500 a year in the First and Second Districts and $22,000 per year in the Third District. The Justices of the Supreme Court (the highest court) are paid $19,500 per year. [Circuit Judge Guyte P. McCord, Jr.]

Q.—Does Florida have District Attorneys?
Not by such title. The State Attorney in this State would probably be the counterpart of the District Attorney in other states.

The prosecuting officers in Florida are:
1. The State Attorney, who serves the grand jury and prosecutes all crimes tried in the Circuit Court.
2. The County Solicitor, who prosecutes all crimes tried in the Courts of Record and the Criminal Courts of Record.
3. The County Prosecuting Attorney, who prosecutes all crimes tried in the County Courts and in the County Judge's Courts. [Justice Stephen C. O'Connell, the Supreme Court]

Q.—What is a Public Defender?

A Public Defender is an attorney of the Florida Bar in good standing, whose duty it is to represent any person who is accused of a non-capital felony when such accused individual cannot afford private counsel of his own choosing, in and after the court of the appropriate jurisdiction has made a prior determination of insolvency. A Public Defender is elected or appointed for each of the judicial circuits. The Public Defender within his own specific circuit cannot act on behalf of the accused until he has been so directed by the court. [Public Defender, Second Circuit]

Q.—Who has to serve on juries in Florida?

Every male citizen over the age of twenty-one years who is a citizen of this state and who has resided in this state for one year and in his county for six months and who is a duly qualified elector of his county and who is selected for such service by the County Commission (or Jury Commission in counties having such) and who has not been convicted of bribery, forgery, perjury, or larceny within this state or under the laws of any other state, government, or country, or who shall not have been convicted within this state of a felony, or under the laws of any other state, government, or country of a crime which, if committed within this state, would be a felony, and who is not under prosecution for any crime; except that the following persons are disqualified from serving: the Governor, the Cabinet officers, the Sheriff or his deputy, the Assessor of Taxes, Collector of Revenue, County Treasurer, Clerks of Courts, Judges, Justices of the Peace, County Commissioners, or United States officials, a person not of sound mind and discretion; and a person interested in any issue to be tried shall not be a juror in that cause.

The following persons may be exempted from jury service if they wish to claim the exemption: persons over sixty-five years of age, persons subject to any bodily infirmity amounting to a disability, attorneys, editorial and news department workers of daily and weekly newspapers and those who gather, prepare, edit, and broadcast news for radio and television stations, officers of colleges or universities, teachers of incorporated academies, teachers of common schools, practicing physicians and surgeons, ministers of the Gospel, Christian Science practitioners and readers, one miller to each grist mill, one ferryman to each licensed ferry, telegraph operators, all superintendents, engineers and train dispatchers of any canal or railroad in operation, ten active members of any hand fire company, six active members of any hose company, either paid or voluntary, twenty active members of any hook and ladder company, all members of the State militia when in active service under call by the Sheriff of the county or by the Governor. [Circuit Judge Guyte P. McCord, Jr.]

Q.—How much is paid for jury duty?
Each juror is paid five dollars per day and five cents per mile for distance traveled to and from court. [Circuit Judge Guyte P. McCord, Jr.]

Q.—Can women serve on juries in Florida?
Yes, women may serve if they register with the Clerk of the Circuit Court for such service. [Circuit Judge Guyte P. McCord, Jr.]

Q.—Who pays the Court Reporter?
The State pays a base salary for reporting criminal cases and for secretarial work for Circuit Judges. In addition to the salary, the Reporter is authorized to sell transcripts of testimony to persons desiring same and to charge litigants for reporting civil cases and anything else they may be privately employed to report. [Circuit Judge Guyte P. McCord, Jr.]

Q.—Are any proceedings of any court secret?
Yes. Grand jury proceedings are conducted in secrecy. The public may be excluded from proceedings in Juvenile Courts and in bastardy proceedings, and records of such proceedings may be sealed by court order. [Justice Stephen C. O'Connell, the Supreme Court]

Q.—Why does a grand jury meet in secret?
The answer to this question is quoted from a handbook entitled *State Grand Juries,* published by the American Bar Association: "Secrecy as to all grand jury proceedings, including not only action upon the indictment or presentment, but the fact that any such matter was considered or any witness called, is of the utmost importance. Thus only can the grand jurors themselves be protected from being subjected to pressure by persons who may be involved in the action of the grand jury. Thus only can persons be prevented from escaping while an indictment against them is under consideration. Thus only can witnesses before the grand jury be prevented from being tampered with, or intimidated, before they testify at the trial. Thus only can such witnesses be encouraged to tell the grand

jury information as to the commission of crime. Thus only can an innocent person who has been improperly subjected to a charge but where the indictment had been dismissed, be saved the disgrace attendant upon the making of such a charge. Note that to achieve the above protection for the grand jury, for the individuals involved, including the witnesses, and for the citizens at large, this pledge of secrecy is paramount and permanent." [Circuit Judge Guyte P. McCord, Jr.]

Q.—Is every indictment prosecuted in the courts?
Not every one. The defendant must be taken into custody before he can be prosecuted. Also, the indictment may be quashed by the court for insufficiency. Or the prosecuting attorney may enter a nolle prosequi, which means that he declines to prosecute the case. Where such is done, this generally means that he does not consider that he has sufficient evidence to present to a trial jury for a conviction. [Circuit Judge Guyte P. McCord, Jr.]

Q.—How much are witnesses in a court trial paid?
Each witness is paid three dollars per day and five cents per mile for distance traveled to and from court. The same mileage is allowed, but only one dollar per day is paid in the Justice of the Peace Courts. [Circuit Judge Guyte P. McCord, Jr.]

Q.—Who pays the Bailiff?
The Sheriff pays the Bailiff. [Circuit Judge Guyte P. McCord, Jr.]

Q.—Who makes up the questions on the Bar Examination?
Florida Bar Examination questions are obtained from three sources:
   1. Bar Examination Service Committee of the National Conference of Bar Examiners.
   2. Florida attorneys employed solely in research and editing capacities.
   3. Law school professors located on campuses outside the State of Florida.
   Source Number 2 is utilized solely for the preparation of questions in the two so-called Florida subjects, Florida Constitutional Law and Florida Rules of Civil Procedure. [Executive Director, Board of Bar Examiners]

Q.—Can a poor person get a lawyer in Florida?
Since the decision of the Supreme Court of the United States in the case of *Gideon* v. *Wainwright,* an indigent person charged with a

felony has available to him the services of the Office of the Public Defender; such an office was established by the 1963 Florida Legislature in each of the sixteen judicial circuits in Florida.

With reference to civil matters, the Florida Bar maintains an active legal aid committee which processes requests for legal services that are directed to the headquarters office of the Florida Bar. This committee over the years has rendered an outstanding service to the public in securing in justifiable instances the volunteer services of a member of the legal profession.

In many of the more populous areas in Florida there have been established legal aid offices, and seven such are presently in operation in Florida. Outside these areas, almost every local bar association, large or small, has a legal aid committee available to receive requests for legal aid services on a gratuitous basis. [Executive Director, the Florida Bar]

Q.—Why do lawyers get half of the damages in a lawsuit?

Historically in the United States it has been the custom in certain types of legal services for the lawyer and the client to agree that the lawyer should be paid on a contingency basis. This contract is designed to compensate the lawyer for his time and services in representing the client. Frequently a contract of this sort is executed by the lawyer and the client because the client is without funds or does not have sufficient funds to compensate a lawyer for what may be months of research, preparation, and trial in handling a personal injury matter. A contract of this type is frequently executed to accommodate the client and not the lawyer. It is safe to say that most lawyers would prefer to be compensated on a time, rather than a contingency, basis for the research they must do to prepare a personal injury action and for the time they must spend in court.

However, lawyers do not customarily get half the damages in a lawsuit, as the question implies. Though this may happen occasionally, it is more common in Florida for a lawyer to take a personal injury action with the agreement that he will receive 25 per cent of the proceeds if the matter is settled prior to trial, and 33 1/3 per cent if it is settled at the trial or afterward. These contracts also specify that in the event the plaintiff is not successful in his suit and the jury or the judge awards no damages, no compensation whatsoever will be paid to the attorney representing the plaintiff. [Executive Director, the Florida Bar]

Q.—If I think a lawyer has charged me too much, can I complain to the Bar Association?

The Florida Bar, which is the official statewide organization of lawyers, has been delegated by the Supreme Court of Florida to investigate acts of alleged unethical conduct by lawyers. The Court's rule authorizes the Florida Bar to make investigations, hold hearings, and enter judgments in disciplinary matters. It also stipulates (in Article XI, Rule 11.02(4) of the Integration Rule of the Florida Bar) that "Controversies as to the amount of fees are not grounds for disciplinary proceedings unless the amount demanded is extortionate or the demand is fraudulent." Thus, the Florida Bar has no jurisdiction in fee disputes unless the amount is extortionate or the demand is fraudulent.

However, several local bar associations have committees to hear disputes between a lawyer and his client concerning fees. Such a committee acts as arbitrator between the lawyer and the client. Before submitting the dispute, the lawyer and the client must agree to accept the committee's decision. The Dade County Bar Association has effectively implemented a program of this type. [Executive Director, the Florida Bar]

Q.—Can a lawyer from another state practice law in Florida?

In Article V, Section 23, of the Florida Constitution, which was adopted by the people of Florida in 1956, the exclusive jurisdiction of the admission of persons to the practice of law and discipline of attorneys was vested with the Supreme Court of Florida. Exercising its exclusive jurisdiction in this area, the Supreme Court announced (in Article II, Section 2, of the Integration Rule of the Florida Bar) the following: "No person shall engage in any way in the practice of law in this state unless such person is an active member of The Florida Bar in good standing except that a practicing attorney of another state, in good standing, who has professional business in a court of record of this state may, upon motion, be permitted to practice for the purpose of such business only, when it is made to appear that he has associated and appearing with him in such business an active member of The Florida Bar."

Accordingly, the answer to the question above is "no" except as set forth in Section 2 quoted above. [Executive Director, the Florida Bar]

Q.—What is contempt of court?

"Contempt of court" is any act which is calculated to embarrass, hinder, or obstruct a court in the administration of justice, or which is calculated to lessen its authority or dignity.

In its broad sense a "contempt" is a disregard of, or disobedience to, the commands of a public authority, legislative or judicial, or an interruption of its proceedings by disorderly behavior or insolent language, in its presence or so near thereto as to disturb its proceedings or impair the respect due to its authority.

Blackstone defines "contempt" as anything that demonstrates a gross want of that regard and respect which, once courts of justice are deprived of, their authority is lost among the people. [Chief Judge, District Court of Appeal, First District]

Q.—Are there any guidelines to what one can say to a judge about a case?

Any attempt outside of a courtroom hearing to influence a judge in the consideration of a case then pending before him is generally deemed to be a contempt of his judicial authority and dignity. Every person has a right to make fair comments and criticisms after a decision is rendered, if they are made in a reasonably courteous manner and for a good purpose, and in so doing one need have no fear of being in contempt. [Justice B. K. Roberts, the Supreme Court]

Q.—How many federal courts are there in Florida?

By act of Congress, Florida is divided into three specific areas, each of which constitutes geographical jurisdiction for one United States District Court. The number of judges in each District is set by Congress according to need.

The twelve southernmost counties comprise the Southern District. Three judges sit in the Southern District. Twenty-three counties from Alachua to Escambia comprise the Northern District of Florida, with one judge. All the other counties on the line from Jacksonville to Tampa comprise the Middle District of Florida. There are four judges currently assigned to this District. Thus, we have three districts with a combined total of eight United States District Judges in Florida.

This is the basic trial unit of the federal court system. Each district is divided into divisions, or places of holding court. For example, in the Northern District of Florida, court is held in Gainesville, Tallahassee, Marianna, and Pensacola.

Appeals from these District Courts are taken to the United States

Court of Appeals, Fifth Circuit, with headquarters in New Orleans. All the District Courts of six Southern states—Texas through Florida —are under the jurisdiction of the Fifth Circuit. This court is comprised of nine judges, any three of whom ordinarily function for the court. Hearings on appeal before the Fifth Circuit are regularly held at Jacksonville, Atlanta, Montgomery, Jackson, New Orleans, and Houston. [U.S. District Judge, Northern District, Florida]

Q.—How do Florida Supreme Court Justices decide how to rule in a case?

An appeal of a case is brought to the State Supreme Court by the lawyer representing the losing party in the trial court, administrative proceedings, or in the District Court of Appeal. In addition to filing his petition or appeal, the attorney also submits to the court a brief in which he informs the court of the facts and issues of the case and of the law which he thinks the court should apply. The other party to the case then has a certain period of time in which to file his brief.

The first question which the court has to decide in most cases is whether or not it has the power or jurisdiction to review the case before it. The court usually makes a preliminary determination of this question before hearing oral arguments on the case. If it determines that it does not have jurisdiction, it may decline to consider the case further, or it may order that the case be transferred to a District Court of Appeal which does have jurisdiction. After the court determines that it does have jurisdiction, the case is set for oral argument. Cases in which the oral argument is heard by all seven of the justices are appeals from judgments imposing the death penalty, appeals from final judgments or decrees directly imposing the death penalty, appeals from final judgments or decrees directly passing upon the validity of a state statute or a federal statute or treaty, appeals from final judgments or decrees construing a controlling provision of the Florida or Federal Constitution, and such other matters as shall be designated by the Chief Justice. Other cases are heard on oral argument by five justices assigned by the Chief Justice. The oral argument which is heard by the Supreme Court is quite different from the hearing of the case before a trial court. No witnesses are present and evidence is not taken, for it is primarily the duty of the Supreme Court to consider only questions involving the law of the case, and they do not decide questions of fact. Usually the parties to the action are not even present at the arguments.

After a case has been argued there is usually a private conference by the members of the court. Following the conference, one of the justices to whom the case has been assigned by the Chief Justice will prepare a written opinion in which the case is discussed and decided. Opinions are written in most of the important cases before the court. After the opinion has been prepared, it is circulated among the other justices for their consideration and approval. If the other justices agree with the opinion, they join in it. If one or more justices disagrees with the opinion, he may dissent, and sometimes a dissenting opinion is written in which the views of the dissenting justices are expressed. Occasionally a justice will agree with the result reached in a case but will feel that the reasons given in the majority opinion are wrong. He may then merely concur or he may write a concurring opinion of his own. Once an opinion has been circulated and agreed to by a majority of the members of the court, it is filed, together with any dissenting and concurring opinions, as the judgment of the court. The judgment of the Supreme Court may result in a final determination of a case or it may result in a case being returned to a trial court for a new trial or for further consideration.

After the opinion of the court has been filed, the losing party has a certain length of time to file a petition for rehearing in which he may point out oversights or omissions in the court's original opinion and ask the court to reconsider its judgment. If no petition for rehearing is filed or if the petition is denied, then the case becomes final as the judgment of the court. If the petition for rehearing is granted, the court may reconsider and either reaffirm or reverse its original decision.

The decisions of the court are printed and published for the use of lawyers and others in the state. These opinions are used as a guide in determining future cases of a similar nature which may arise in the courts of the State. [Chief Justice, Supreme Court]

Q.—When can I watch the Supreme Court?
You are entitled at any time during the office hours of the court, which are from 8:30 in the morning until 5:00 in the afternoon, to be present at any of the public places in the building and to observe any action taken except at the private conferences of the court following the argument of cases or in the private conferences of the court every Monday morning for the determination of questions on opinions which have been prepared or are in the process of prepara-

tion. These involve cases which have been argued but not disposed of and it is easy to see the necessity for these conferences to be entirely confidential until the opinion is filed in the Clerk's office. [Chief Justice, Supreme Court]

Q.—Do the Justices actually write the opinions themselves, or does the Clerk?
Justices of the Supreme Court write their own opinions. In this task, each Justice is assisted by a research assistant. The research assistants draw together the findings of courts in this and other states on the legal questions presented in the case assigned to their judge. They serve, in a manner of speaking, as the Justice's eyes and legs. By doing this basic chore of assembling the available information, the research assistants make it possible for the judges to write better opinions faster. The Clerk of the Supreme Court is its recording officer.

Q.—Can anyone use the law library in the Supreme Court building?
The Supreme Court has limited its library to "members of the bar of the Supreme Court, to members of the Legislature, to law officers of the Executive and other departments of the state, and to such other persons as, by special permission of the court, may be allowed to use the library." The library has some 51,000 volumes but its specialized nature serves to confine its use almost entirely to readers specified in the court's rule. Only Justices of the Supreme Court may take books from the library; others may consult the books there.

Q.—What is the bell in front of the Supreme Court Building?
This replica of the Liberty Bell was one of 53 cast in France and given to the United States government by American copper, steel, and refining companies. In turn, the bells were given to the states by the Secretary of the Treasury as a symbol of the Savings Bonds Independence Drive of 1950. The Florida bell is sounded on patriotic occasions.

Q.—Can I appeal a traffic court conviction in muncipal courts?
Yes. Florida Statutes 932.52(1) reads as follows: "Appeals from municipal courts.—Any person convicted of any offense in any municipal court in this state may appeal from the judgment of such court to the circuit court of the county in which the conviction took place." [Municipal Judge, City of Tallahassee]

Q.—What does it cost to "take a case to the Supreme Court"?
The filing fee charged by the Clerk of the Supreme Court is $25. The rules require that a certified transcript of the proceeding in the court being reviewed must be filed with the Supreme Court and this can cost from $10 to many thousands of dollars, depending upon the size of the transcript. The average cost is about $100. The rules also require a brief (written argument) to be filed which could possibly be done by the party without a lawyer, but with about the same skill as a layman trying to remove an appendix in a hospital. It is better to have counsel and that would run on an average of about $250. If done by the litigant, there would be no cost. [Justice B. K. Roberts, the Supreme Court]

Q.—How is the Chief Justice of the Supreme Court selected?
"The Chief Justice of the Supreme Court shall be chosen by the members of the court [from membership of the court] and shall serve for a term of two years. . . . During a vacancy or whenever the Chief Justice is unable to act for any reason, the justice longest in continuous service and able to act shall act as Chief Justice." Article V, Section 4, Constitution of Florida. [Justice B. K. Roberts, the Supreme Court]

Q.—What is a subpoena? Who can issue one? Is there any subpoena which can be ignored?
There are different kinds of subpoenas. However, generally, they may be cumulatively defined as a process or mandatory writ directing one or more persons to appear and give testimony, and/or produce papers, documents, etc., before a court or magistrate therein named and at a time therein mentioned. Any court of competent jurisdiction over the parties and/or the subject matter may properly order the issuance of a subpoena. The Clerk of the Court executes the court's order and actually issues the subpoena. Except in unusual circumstances, a subpoena may not be ignored. In no instance *should* a subpoena be ignored. [Attorney General]

Q.—Is there anyone in Florida who cannot be subpoenaed?
Generally, no person is immune from the subpoena process. Again, unusual circumstances may exist which would immunize a person from a subpoena. [Attorney General]

Q.—Does Florida have the death penalty?
Yes. Death by electrocution has been the method since January 1, 1924. In prior years the death penalty was carried out by hanging.

Q.—Can the Governor commute a death sentence?

The Governor, acting as one of a majority of the Pardon Board, can commute a death sentence. The other members of the Pardon Board are the Secretary of State, Attorney General, Comptroller, and Commissioner of Agriculture. He cannot do this by himself, nor can the other members of the Pardon Board do this without his agreement. The Governor can delay the execution of the death sentence by withholding his signature from the death warrant, and no one can force the Governor to sign. This would leave the burden to his successor in office.

Q.—What is the difference in parole, probation, and pardon?

Parole is a conditional release granted a prisoner after he has served a portion of his sentence in a penal institution. Parole has no connection with forgiveness, nor is it designed as a reward for good conduct in the institution. Its basic purpose is to bridge the transition between the closely ordered life within a prison and the freedom of normal community living. A parolee may be arrested and reimprisoned without trial for breach of good conduct during the unserved portion of his sentence. In Florida, parole is administered by the Parole Commission, an agency directed by three commissioners.

Probation is the postponement of final judgment or verdict in a criminal case, giving the offender an opportunity to start life afresh, often on conditions imposed by the court and under the guidance and supervision of an officer of the court. The probationer, if he passes successfully through the period of supervision set by the court, need never undergo imprisonment at all.

Pardon involves forgiveness. It is an executive act of grace, granted in Florida by the Pardon Board, a Cabinet board headed by the Governor. Pardons are of two kinds, full and conditional. A person receiving a full pardon has been restored to free membership in the community without further penal liability for the wrong pardoned. Conditional pardon is somewhat akin to parole, particularly when granted after a period of imprisonment. A pardon may be granted at any time, either before, after, or during imprisonment. Pardons often are granted after the service of sentence to restore the civil rights that have been forfeited upon conviction.

Commutation is another expression of executive clemency, although this power is in some instances exercised by the courts. Commutation consists of the substitution of a lesser punishment for that which was originally imposed, such as a fine instead of imprisonment.

Suspended sentence is a variation of probation, the significant difference being that a suspended sentence is, as a rule, not accompanied by supervision. [Chairman, Parole Commission]

Q.—How many different kinds of law enforcement officers does Florida have?

There are a myriad of law enforcement officers in Florida. Basically, Florida has officers on three levels: state, county, and municipal. On the state level alone there are a number of kinds of law enforcement officers such as Florida Highway Patrolmen, Game Wardens, etc. [Attorney General]

Q.—What is the difference between a sheriff and a chief of police?

The basic difference between these two officers is that a sheriff is an elected county official and a chief of police is a municipal police officer. Also, the jurisdiction of a sheriff extends further than that of a chief of police. [Attorney General]

Q.—Who is the chief law enforcement officer in Florida?

Under the Florida Constitution the Governor is designated as the Chief Executive and the Chief Magistrate of the State of Florida and is vested with the responsibility to see that all laws are properly executed. [Attorney General]

Q.—Do city and county police generally cooperate, or is there competition between them?

Generally, there is excellent cooperation among city and county law enforcement officers. The old days of competition have given way to an era of cooperation, and except in isolated individual instances, relationships are very good. [General Counsel, Florida Sheriffs' Association]

Q.—Do all sheriffs make the same salary?

No. Generally, salaries vary depending upon the size of the county, and are set primarily by the legislative delegations through special or population acts. [General Counsel, Florida Sheriffs' Association]

Q.—What are constables, and how many of them are there?

The constable is the enforcement officer of the Courts of Justices of the Peace. The number of such courts varies from time to time, as the Constitution allows the Legislature to establish or abolish these, subject to the favoring vote of the people in the county affected.

Q.—Does Florida have a State police force?
No. The Governor has the power, in the protection of the public welfare, to declare an emergency and call upon the "military forces of the state or any other law enforcement agency, state or county" to enforce whatever rules and regulations he believes the situation requires.

In the exercise of this extraordinary authority, the Governor has assembled troopers of the Highway Patrol, agents of the Conservation Department, agents of the Beverage Department, guards from the Division of Corrections, and deputies from the office of the County Sheriff, under a unified command.

This special mobilization was called a State police force by newsmen but it was not that in the usual meaning of a regular law enforcement agency such as some states have.

Q.—Can the Highway Patrol enforce any laws besides traffic laws?
Highway Patrolmen are limited generally to arrests for offenses of any nature involving the public roads. They may apprehend fugitives from justice. They are required to maintain public peace by preventing violence on the highways. The Executive Board of the Department of Public Safety (the Governor and the Cabinet) may authorize patrolmen to assist other law enforcement officers in quelling riots, guarding prisoners, and policing disaster areas.

Q.—What is the jurisdiction of the Florida Sheriffs' Bureau?
The Bureau operates a Criminal Analysis Laboratory, trains law enforcement officers, transmits police information by teletype and otherwise, seeks coordination of law enforcement practices, and, only upon the request of the Sheriff of the county involved, investigates a specific crime. The Bureau is managed by the Governor, the Attorney General, and five sheriffs selected by the Governor.

Q.—How many private detectives are there in Florida? Are they regulated by the State?
Under the provisions of Chapter 63-340, Laws of Florida, Acts of 1963, the following number of licenses in the categories as indicated have been issued: 90 private investigative agency licenses; 34 watchman, guard, or patrolman agency licenses; 105 detective licenses; 18 watchman, guard, or patrolman contractors. (Several applications are presently pending in each of these categories.)

An accurate count of private detectives in the State of Florida is not now possible because: (1) An agency is not compelled by law to tell us the number of private detectives or watchmen that it employs; (2) many private detectives employed solely by one employer need not be licensed; (3) there is no accurate number of those who have not complied with the law, and who do not fit in either of the above two categories; (4) there undoubtedly are many unlicensed persons within the state whose identities are still unknown to us. The law regulating and providing for the licensing of private detectives has only been in effect a little over two months and we are still in the process of gathering information in order that we can contact all those persons involved under the requirements of this law. [Secretary of State]

Q.—How many agents of the Federal Bureau of Investigation normally work in Florida?

Security regulations prohibit furnishing information relative to the number of Special Agents who normally work in Florida.

You may be interested in the fact that there are three FBI field divisions in this state. Headquarters for the northern portion is at 414 United States Courthouse and Post Office Building, Jacksonville; for the middle portion of Florida at 1224 South Dale Mabry Highway, Tampa; and the southern portion of Florida at 3915 Biscayne Boulevard, Miami. [Special Agent in Charge, North Florida Division, Federal Bureau of Investigation]

Q.—Who may make an arrest in Florida?

Generally, any person, and of course any law enforcement officer may make an arrest in Florida under the proper circumstances. [Attorney General]

Q.—Can the Sheriff hire anyone he wants as his deputy?

There are no basic limitations to a Sheriff employing anyone as a Deputy Sheriff. Minor prerequisites are necessary, however, such as the Deputy Sheriff providing a bond pursuant to Section 30.09, Florida Statutes. [Attorney General]

Q.—Is wire tapping legal in Florida?

Section 822.10, Florida Statutes, in effect, provides for a fine or imprisonment for wire tapping without the consent of the owner. The primary purpose of this statute is to protect the property of the owners thereof. There are federal laws prohibiting the same. [Attorney General]

Q.—Is anyone, including legislators during a session of the Legislature, immune from arrest in Florida?

Generally, no one, not even legislators during a session of the Legislature, is immune from arrest in Florida. This answer, of course, assumes that the arrest is in all respects a valid arrest. [Attorney General]

Voting and Running
for Public Office

Q.—Who may register to vote in Florida?

Any citizen of the United States who is twenty-one or over, a resident of the State for one year and of the county for six months, is eligible to register with the Supervisor of Registration when the books are open. [Secretary of State]

Q.—When can I register to vote in Florida?

The books close thirty days before a primary or general election and remain closed five days after the primary or general election. In several of the small counties, the Supervisor of Registration does not keep the office open each weekday, but gives notice of the days it will be open. Most offices are kept open each weekday and, for thirty days prior to closing the books for the first primary, the office is open two nights each week unless County Commissioners direct otherwise. [Secretary of State]

Q.—Where can I register to vote in Florida?

Registrations may be made at the office of the Supervisor of Registration. Members of the armed services and their spouses who are residents of Florida may register absentee. [Secretary of State]

*Q.—Does a voter have to register as a member of a political party
in order to register to vote?*

No, a person qualified (mainly by age and residence) to vote may register without declaring himself to be a member of any political party. Such party-less voters may participate only in the November general elections for the filling of public offices. The primaries are reserved for the selection by party members of nominees. The names of these nominees appear on the general election ballot.

70

Q.—Do people sometimes have to register in two places—for city and county elections, for instance?

Yes. There is provision, however, for cities to adopt the county permanent registration system and use the county books in their elections. [Secretary of State]

Q.—Who sets the hours that a Supervisor of Registration has to keep the office open?

The law makes provision for hours the books are open; however, County Commissioners may authorize the Supervisor to keep books open for less time. [Secretary of State]

Q.—Are voting machines used in all counties?

At last count by the Office of the Secretary of State, 49 of the 67 counties were using voting machines. Use in some precincts of a county on a trial basis is authorized, but once adopted, voting machines supplant paper ballots countywide.

Q.—Who watchdogs the voting machines?

The Supervisors of Registration are custodians of voting machines. Before machines are prepared for any election, the Supervisor shall mail written notice to the Chairman of the County Executive Committee of the principal parties, stating the time and place where the machines will be prepared, at which time one representative of each political party is afforded an opportunity to see that the machines are in proper condition. The Secretary of State also has the authority to examine the operation of voting machines. [Secretary of State]

Q.—Is there any way to "cheat" on election returns?

Most counties use voting machines. The machines are locked immediately when the polls are closed. Should any question arise about the returns, the results can again be checked on the machine. The returns are made in the presence of watchers or other persons lawfully in the polling place. There is no way that we know of. [Secretary of State]

Q.—Can I run for public office in Florida?

This depends on the office. There are residence requirements for certain offices. [Secretary of State]

Q.—Who can run for Governor of Florida?

Anyone can run for Governor who is a qualified elector and, at the time of the election, has been a citizen of the United States for ten years and a resident of Florida for five years.

Q.—How much does it cost to run for Governor of Florida?
Some idea of the cost of running may be gained from the reports of candidates for Governor to the Secretary of State under the State's "Who gave it, who got it" campaign expense law. Haydon Burns said his double-primary campaign for the Democratic nomination in 1964 cost $750,332.

Q.—Who can run for the Legislature?
To run for the Legislature, one must be a duly qualified elector in the county and district from which he is chosen. [Secretary of State]

Q.—Who can run for County Commissioner in Florida?
Any qualified elector who resides in the County Commissioner's district may run for that County Commissioner's office. [Secretary of State]

Q.—What must a candidate pay in qualifying fee to run for public office?
The qualifying fee is 5 per cent of the first year's salary of the office at the time of the election.

Q.—How do you get an absentee ballot?
An absentee ballot may be obtained by applying to the Supervisor of Registration at any time during the forty-five days preceding any election, but not later than 5:00 P.M. of the fifth day preceding such election. [Secretary of State]

Q.—Has there ever been a recall election in Florida?
There is no provision in our law for recall of elected State or county officials at the present time. [Secretary of State]

Q.—Has a woman ever been elected to statewide office in Florida?
Yes. Mrs. Mamie Eaton Greene of Monticello was twice elected statewide as a member of the Railroad Commission. She had been appointed to the Commission on March 23, 1927, upon the death of her first husband, R. L. (Bob) Eaton. She was elected in 1928 for the remaining two years of his term, and then elected in 1930 for a four-year term in her own right. Mrs. Greene was defeated for re-election in 1934.

Q.—What is a freeholder?

The term is used generally in elections pledging the revenue from property taxes to the retirement of bonds for public improvements. A freeholder is a person in that area who possesses the ordinary requirements of a voter but also either owns or is buying land there. Generally, only freeholders are allowed to vote on the issuance of bonds because they are, in effect, voting whether they are willing to pay additional taxes for the improvement.

Q.—What is a referendum?

A referendum is an election offering the voters an opportunity to express themselves on some public question. Thus, the problem has been "referred" by a governing body to the people. For example, "Shall our county operate a library?"

Q.—What is a primary election?

A primary election is one conducted by a political party for the purpose of selecting its nominees. If no candidate receives a majority in the first primary, the two candidates getting the most votes are automatically entered in the second or "runoff" primary. Only the registered members of that political party can vote in its primaries. Everyone qualified by registration may vote in the general election. It is not necessary to declare an affiliation with a political party to register, but nonaligned voters—usually known as "independents"—are limited to the general election. Incidentally, voters participating in a general election can "write in," on voting machine or paper ballot, the name of some other person if they find the nominees of both parties unacceptable. It is this "write in" privilege that makes it necessary to list the names of all party nominees on the general election ballot even when a nominee may be unopposed. Presently, regular primary elections are held in May; general elections in November.

Q.—How can I get to be a poll watcher?

A poll watcher must be designated by a candidate for election, and this designation must be in written notice to the county Supervisor of Registration at least 14 days in advance of any primary or election. [Secretary of State]

Q.—What other jobs are available on election days and how can I get one?

Each precinct polling place is staffed by inspectors, clerks, and special deputy sheriffs. The size of this force depends upon the number of electors registered to vote at the particular precinct polling place. The inspectors and clerks are appointed by the County Commissioner in whose district the polling place is situated. The special deputies are appointed by the Sheriff of the county.

Q.—Does Florida have preferential presidential primaries?
Yes, they are held in May in conjunction with the regular party runoff primary.

The Public Schools

Q.—Who runs the schools in each county?
Florida law specifically provides that, "All public schools conducted within the county shall be under the direction and control of the county board [County Board of Public Instruction] with the county superintendent as executive officer. . . ." [State Superintendent of Public Instruction]

Q.—Is the County Superintendent of Public Instruction elected or appointed?
The County Superintendent of Public Instruction is an elective official in a majority of Florida counties. However, the Florida Constitution has been amended to allow some counties to appoint their superintendent. Appointed superintendents are now serving in Dade, Sarasota, Pinellas, Orange, Brevard, Collier, and Indian River counties. [State Superintendent of Public Instruction]

Q.—Can I attend a County School Board meeting?
School Board meetings are public; therefore, anyone may attend them. [State Superintendent of Public Instruction]

Q.—Are School Board members paid? Trustees?
All counties pay monthly salaries to Board members. The amounts vary. Trustees serve without pay. [State Superintendent of Public Instruction]

Q.—Who can run for the School Board?
A member of the County Board of Public Instruction must be a qualified elector of the county which he serves and must be a resident of the county board member resident district from which he is elected. Although he must reside in a specific district, he must run for office countywide. [State Superintendent of Public Instruction]

Q.—What is the difference in School Boards and School Trustees?
The responsibility for the organization and control of the schools of a
county is vested in the County Board of Public Instruction. The
powers of the Trustees are supervisory in nature and are not administrative or controlling powers. The Trustees advise with the County
Superintendent and the County Board and make recommendations
with respect to the general welfare and need of the schools of the
county. The major responsibility of the Trustees is that of nominating
and dismissing members of the instructional staff. In the employment
of instructional personnel, the County Superintendent recommends
to the Trustees; the Trustees nominate to the County Board; and the
County Board appoints. [State Superintendent of Public Instruction]

Q.—Why is a school district in Florida the whole county?
The basic governmental organization within the State of Florida is
the sixty-seven county units. Practically all of the governmental agencies, other than State agencies, are organized on the county-level
structure. Before 1947, the year that the Minimum Foundation Program was enacted into law, the individual counties were divided into
school districts of varying sizes. This caused many inefficient and
illogical patterns of operations, particularly in regard to the number
of pupils within a given district and the taxable wealth relationship.
Since 1947 each county constitutes a single school district, which has
brought about many advantages, such as centralized or countywide
planning, increased efficiency in business operations, a uniform
countywide tax rate for schools. One of the major advantages is that
now all of the taxable wealth within a given county is available to
support the total educational program regardless of where the child
lives or the wealth appears geographically. [State Superintendent of
Public Instruction]

Q.—What is school millage?
A mill is the ratio of one to one thousand. One mill of tax is, then, a
tax of one dollar for each one thousand dollars of taxable wealth. In
Florida the School Board may, by resolution, levy a tax rate of not
less than three mills nor more than ten mills. In addition to this
millage levy, the voters may approve a tax not to exceed ten mills,
making a total of twenty mills as a maximum countywide tax for
the operation of schools within a county system. The people may vote
a countywide bond issue for school facilities and the tax necessary
to provide the debt service for this bond issue is levied in addition to

the millage required for the operation of schools. Thus a county may have twenty mills plus the millage required to retire the bond issue. [State Superintendent of Public Instruction]

Q.—Why does Florida have a teacher shortage?
Public school enrollment in Florida has doubled in the last ten years. More than 5,000 new teachers are needed each year for new pupils and to replace teachers leaving the profession. Florida's standards for new teachers are high. More than 99 per cent have college degrees. Florida's education program places emphasis on mathematics, science, and other subjects for which the national teacher supply is limited. Local teacher training institutions provide less than a third of the new teachers needed each year. All of these factors contribute to the shortage of teachers. [State Superintendent of Public Instruction]

Q.—Can an out-of-state teacher get a teaching certificate easily in Florida?
The graduate of a standard four-year college, whether in-state or out-of-state, is eligible for a Florida teaching certificate provided the college will recommend him for such certificate. [State Superintendent of Public Instruction]

Q.—How does teacher pay in Florida rank with the other states?
The average salary paid teachers in Florida is the highest in the Southeast. In 1962-63 Florida ranked twenty-fifth among the fifty states. This position should be improved as a result of the salary increases granted by the 1963 Florida Legislature. [State Superintendent of Public Instruction]

Q.—Does Florida have public school kindergartens?
Participation in the State kindergarten program is optional. Twelve counties with a kindergarten enrollment of 5,700 participated in 1963. To be eligible for a State kindergarten program, a county must contribute to the cost of the program and meet certain standards as to qualification of teachers and adequate physical facilities.

Counties having kindergarten programs are Alachua, Calhoun, Citrus, Dixie, Flagler, Gilchrist, Glades, Jefferson, Liberty, Manatee, Volusia, and Washington. Dade County has a limited locally supported kindergarten program. [State Superintendent of Public Instruction]

Q.—Are textbooks free in Florida?

Textbooks are provided without cost to students in grades one through twelve in the public schools. [State Superintendent of Public Instruction]

Q.—Who selects the textbooks in Florida?

After a committee of professional educators and lay citizens evaluates and recommends the textbooks to be adopted, the State Textbook Purchasing Board, which is the Governor and the Cabinet, makes the final decision on the textbooks to be purchased for use in the public schools of the state. [State Superintendent of Public Instruction]

Q.—Is school bus service available to every child in Florida?

School bus service is available to virtually all rural and suburban public school pupils who live beyond walking distance from the schools they are expected to attend. Walking distance is defined by law as less than two miles. In cities, school bus service is available for most public school pupils not within walking distance of their schools, but is sometimes not provided for high school students when city bus service is available. [State Superintendent of Public Instruction]

Q.—Are children of non-residents permitted to attend Florida schools?

A pupil whose parents or guardian are non-residents of Florida must pay a tuition fee of $50 at the time of enrollment. The fee is payable only for a school year and is not required if the pupil later transfers to another county during the same school year. (No refund is made. The official receipt is evidence of the prior payment of the tuition fee.) No tuition fee is charged if the parent or guardian (a) is in military service, (b) is a civilian employee and the cost of the child's education is provided in part or in whole by federal subsidy, (c) is a migratory agricultural worker, or (d) if the pupil is attending school under a special exchange program approved by the County Board.

A person to be considered a resident of Florida must: (a) have lived in Florida one year or longer, or (b) have purchased a home in Florida which is occupied by him as his residence, or (c) have filed a manifestation of domicile in the county in which the child is enrolled. [State Superintendent of Public Instruction]

Q.—How old must a child be before he drops out of school?

A pupil is required to attend school until he attains the age of sixteen years unless he is granted a certificate of exemption from school attendance. [State Superintendent of Public Instruction]

Q.—At what age may a child enter public school?
A child who will attain the age of six years on or before January 1 of the school year in which he enrolls may be admitted to the first grade provided he enrolls during the first month of the school term. [State Superintendent of Public Instruction]

Q.—Why don't Florida grammar schools have libraries?
Many Florida elementary schools have libraries. Some elementary schools do not provide libraries because they do not have the funds to employ a librarian. All junior and senior high schools have libraries. [State Superintendent of Public Instruction]

Q.—What is the Minimum Foundation?
The Minimum Foundation Program is a formula by which the State and the counties share in the cost of equal minimum educational opportunities for every child. It is based on the premise that every child in Florida, regardless of the wealth of the county in which he lives, deserves equal minimum opportunities for an adequate education. Financial support for the Minimum Foundation Program varies with school population, with the professional training and experience of teachers, and with the breadth of the program maintained in a county. [State Superintendent of Public Instruction]

Q.—Will Florida high schools prepare my child for top eastern colleges?
The increasing number of Florida public high-school students who are achieving success in the so-called prestige colleges, the impressive scores Florida students have consistently made on nationally compared achievement tests—including the College Entrance Examination Board tests—and the large number of national scholarships being awarded annually to Florida students speak well for the quality of instruction provided in Florida public schools; but entrance to the leading colleges in the United States depends more on the individual and his capabilities than it does on the secondary school he attends. In determining admissibility, it is the quality of the individual candidate, not his school, which is of primary concern. If he has the necessary academic ability, has followed a carefully planned program and has performed well in his high school, shows more than ordinary promise, and can obtain from his high school a character recom-

mendation, the Florida student will encounter no difficulty in competing for admission to the best of colleges. [State Superintendent of Public Instruction]

Q.—Does Florida have adult education programs?
Yes, Florida does have adult education programs. They are of two major types: general adult education, and adult vocational education. General adult education provides opportunities for adults in the following areas: literacy and elementary education, high school completion, citizenship and public affairs education, education for aging, and cultural and liberal education. General adult education is available for all individuals beyond sixteen years of age who have legally left school, is offered at times most convenient to the participants, and is presented in the community public schools.

Adult vocational education provides opportunities for adults to learn necessary skills for obtaining employment or to improve skills needed for job advancement. Course work is available in the area of: industrial education, technical education, distributive education, business education, agricultural education, and home economics education. Adult vocational education is available for all individuals beyond sixteen years of age who have legally left school, is offered at times most convenient to the participants, and is presented in the community public schools. [State Superintendent of Public Instruction]

Q.—Does the State have a special program for educating handicapped children?
Through Florida's Exceptional Child Program many county school systems provide educational programs for all types of handicapped children. Usually the most comprehensive programs are in the more populous areas. [State Superintendent of Public Instruction]

Q.—Does the State provide for retarded children?
Through the Exceptional Child Program, all but four of the sixty-seven county school systems have one or more classes for retarded children. Twenty-two of these counties also have classes for severely mentally retarded children. In view of the rapid growth of Florida there is a long waiting list for classes in many communities so that it is suggested that interested people contact the Superintendent in the respective area where they wish to settle to be assured that an opening would be available. Florida also has an outstanding residential pro-

gram for the retarded and a number of private schools, both residential and day schools, located throughout the state.

Q.—Is there a special program for exceptionally bright children?
There are a few county school systems that have programs for exceptionally bright children but most planning and provisions for these children are initiated by the local school system.

Q.—When did Florida begin its free public school system?
Florida's first free public school law was passed in 1849. [State Librarian]

Q.—How did Florida finance its first public schools?
Schools were initially financed by distribution to the counties of interest on the State School Fund, into which were paid proceeds of the sales of sixteenth-section lands, the 5 per cent received from the United States on the sale of public land in Florida, and proceeds of escheated estates and of the sale of wrecked and derelict property. In 1851, counties were authorized to levy a tax on both real and personal property for the support of common schools. [State Librarian]

CHAPTER
SEVEN

Higher Learning and Culture

Q.—How many State universities are there?
Presently, there are five public universities: the University of Florida
at Gainesville; the Florida State University and Florida Agricultural
and Mechanical University at Tallahassee; the University of South
Florida at Tampa; and Florida Atlantic University at Boca Raton.
Still other degree-granting institutions have been authorized for Pensacola and for east-central Florida in the vicinity of Orlando.

Q.—Who runs the State universities?
Florida's public universities are supervised by the State Board of
Regents and, in turn, by the State Board of Education, composed of
the Governor, Secretary of State, Attorney General, Treasurer, and
Superintendent of Public Instruction. Also, the Legislature has a
hand in making policies for execution by the Board of Education, the
Board of Regents, and the presidents and staffs of the individual
institutions.

There are nine members of the Board of Regents. Regents are
appointed by the Governor, with the concurrence of the Board of
Education and the consent of the Senate. Required to have been
citizens of Florida for at least ten years prior to appointment, Regents
are selected from "the state at large, representative of the geographical areas." Regents enjoy the longest term the Constitution
allows a State official: nine years. (The Board of Regents replaced
in 1965 the Board of Control, whose members' terms had been
limited to four years.)

Q.—What are admission standards for State universities?
To be admitted to a State university a student must: be a graduate
of an accredited high school; have a satisfactory high school record,
including a C average or better in academic subjects; and stand in

82

the upper 40 per cent in the Florida Twelfth Grade Testing Program. Applicants who meet the first two requirements, but who attain scores on the Twelfth Grade Tests between the 40th and 60th percentiles can be considered for admission on an individual basis.

Out-of-state students are admitted if they meet requirements equivalent to the above. [Director, Board of Regents]

Q.—Can adults register for classes at a State university without working for a degree?

Yes, if they are qualified for admission and for the courses they elect. [Director, Board of Regents]

Q.—Can residents of Florida use the libraries at the State universities if they are not enrolled?

Florida residents may use the libraries at the State universities, but they must secure special permits in order to take books from the library. Applications for such permits should be made to the Director of Libraries of the institution in question. [Director, Board of Regents]

Q.—Do any of the universities have specialties, or is the curriculum about the same at all of them?

The policy of the Board of Regents is that our universities shall serve the needs of Florida students without unnecessary duplication. The result of this policy is that in those areas where demand is great, all institutions offer courses. Examples of curricula that are similar in all institutions are teacher education, business administration, and of course, basic studies (general or liberal education for freshmen and sophomores). Areas of lesser need (in terms of numbers of potential students) or areas in which expense, buildings, equipment, or staffing problems are great, are distributed among the universities. Thus we have medicine at the University of Florida, music (as a school) at Florida State University, engineering (applied) at University of Florida, and engineering science at Florida State University, agriculture at the University of Florida, and so on. [Director, Board of Regents]

Q.—How much does it cost to attend one of the State universities? Is tuition about the same at each?

The basic costs of attending the State universities are:
Florida A. & M.
    Tuition—$90.00 per trimester
    Room and board—approximately $238.00 per trimester
    Out-of-state students pay tuition of $175.00 per trimester.

University of Florida
  Tuition—$113.00 per trimester
  Room and board—$285.00 per trimester
  Out-of-state students pay tuition of $288.00 per trimester.
University of South Florida
  Tuition—$113.00 per trimester
  Room and board—$325.00 per trimester
  Out-of-state students pay tuition of $288.00 per trimester.
Florida State University
  Tuition—$113.00 per trimester
  Room and board—$280.00 per trimester
  Out-of-state students pay tuition of $288.00 per trimester.

The above expenses do not include cost of books, laundry, special laboratory fees, etc., all of which vary with individual students. [Director, Board of Regents]

Q.—Can anyone enroll in the junior colleges?
Florida's community junior colleges offer educational programs in freshman and sophomore courses, in occupational courses, and in adult education. Students who are admitted to credit programs must have completed their high school work or its equivalent. Those enrolling in non-credit programs do not have to meet this requirement. [State Superintendent of Public Instruction]

Q.—What are the admission standards for a junior college?
Since the community junior colleges have responsibilities in several areas of education, it is essential to report admission requirements in terms of the programs a student wishes to take. *Generally speaking, a student must be a graduate of an accredited high school in order to be admitted to a junior college.* However, this graduation may not be enough to achieve admission in certain specialized programs such as nursing or data processing technology where other more stringent requirements may be found. On the other hand, no particular level of previous education may be necessary to be admitted to some of the vocational skills or non-credit courses which are offered.

In other words, the usual admission requirement to a junior college, but not to special programs within the college, is graduation from high school or its equivalent with the provision that anyone may be admitted if he can demonstrate that he will profit by the experience and has achieved the approval of the junior college president. [State Superintendent of Public Instruction]

Q.—Are the junior colleges part of the school system or the college system?

The junior colleges are defined by law as higher education at the local level. They are under the immediate control of those local Boards of Public Instruction which have been specifically approved by the State Board of Education to operate junior colleges. State level coordination is provided through the State Junior College Board's recommendations to the Board of Education, which is the State agency responsible for all levels of education. Liaison between the junior colleges and the universities is provided through the Board of Education and through a professional committee representing high schools, junior colleges, and universities.

Junior colleges are a part of the college system in terms of their programs; they are a part of the local public school systems in terms of their operation. [State Superintendent of Public Instruction]

Q.—Does football make money for the State universities?

This is a complicated question to attempt to answer. To isolate the monies directly chargeable to or derived from football from the complicated financial structure of university operations would be a very difficult task. Perhaps it can be answered in this way: Football does not make a profit, but it does generate an important part of the money needed to support the athletic plant and program of the institution. [Director, Board of Regents]

Q.—Does the State give any financial support to private colleges?

Yes, in the form of research grants, race-track scholarship funds, and support for the medical school at the University of Miami. [Director, Board of Regents]

Q.—Can anyone in Florida check out a book from the State Library?

Any resident of Florida may borrow a book from the State Library at Tallahassee through his public library, or directly if there is no public library in his community. [State Librarian]

Q.—How many museums does the State of Florida operate?

The Ringling Museum is the only art museum operated by the State of Florida. The State also operates the Florida State Museum of Natural History in Gainesville. [Director, Ringling Museums]

Q.—Who can borrow works of art from the Ringling Museum?

The Board of Trustees of the Ringling Museum may make temporary loans not to exceed six months' duration to ". . . art museums, and institutions of higher learning, and the executive mansion in Tallahassee." [Director, Ringling Museums]

Q.—Does the State of Florida do anything to protect historical sites and old houses?
Unless the historical sites or old houses belong to the Florida Board of Parks and Historic Memorials, no effort is made to protect them. Those historical sites and houses within our jurisdiction naturally receive the protection and maintenance of our Park Rangers. [Chief of Information and Education, Park Service]

Q.—Does Florida have a State medical college?
The State has a medical college at the University of Florida in Gainesville and contributes to the support of the medical college at the privately operated University of Miami.

Q.—Does Florida have a State dental college?
No.

Q.—Does Florida have a law school?
There are law schools at two public universities, the University of Florida at Gainesville and Florida A. & M. University at Tallahassee. Two privately operated institutions also have law schools; the University of Miami's is on its campus at Coral Gables and Stetson University's is at St. Petersburg. Graduates of Florida law schools no longer enjoy the diploma privilege, but gain admission to practice only through taking a separate Supreme Court-supervised examination.

Q.—What is the Florida State Symphony?
The Florida State Symphony and the Florida State Opera were created by the 1963 Legislature. No appropriation was made at that time. The Symphony and the Opera are administered by the Florida State University School of Music. Services of the orchestra and opera may be made available, at the discretion of the Administrative Committee, to civic groups and public schools.

Q.—What is the role of the Florida Arts Commission?
The Commission, an advisory offshoot of the Board of Commissioners of State Institutions, has the opportunity to counsel the State government in the fine arts field generally. Specifically, the Commission endeavors to promote the appropriate decoration of the Capitol and

other public buildings. It is composed of nine citizens with a special interest in the orderly development of the artistic and cultural resources of the state.

Q.—What is the Florida Arts Festival?

By proclamation of the Governor, this is a continuing campaign to bring Florida cultural activities to the attention of Floridians and visitors. A 1962-63 survey by the Development Commission disclosed the existence of numerous artistic activities which were largely escaping public notice even in their home communities. Through the coordination of the Florida Arts Council, advertisements, a printed free calendar of events, and other promotional efforts have been used to publicize events ranging from art exhibits to symphony concerts, from hootenannies to ballets.

Land and Sea and Sky

Q.—How much land does the State own?
The Trustees of the Internal Improvement Fund, as of July 18, 1963, own 335,928.93 acres of public domain lands, not submerged lands, and the State Board of Education, as of the same date, is owner of 81,174.69 acres of public domain lands. Both the Trustees and the Board of Education have authority to sell these lands, but only a small percentage is open for application to purchase. [Director, Trustees of the Internal Improvement Fund]

Q.—Who issues permits for oil drilling in Florida?
The Board of Conservation issues these permits after review and recommendation of the Oil and Gas Division Administrator, who is the Director of the Division of Geology. [State Geologist]

Q.—Does the State protect archeological finds?
According to the Rules and Regulations of the Florida Park Service, section 265-1.03(4) REMOVAL OF PROPERTY: "No person shall dig, move, mar, deface or remove from any Park area any beach sand, gravel or minerals, whether submerged or not, or any soil, rock stalactites, stalagmites, artifacts, relics, stones, trees, shrubs, or plants, downtimber or other wood or materials, or make any excavation by tool, equipment, blasting, or other means or agency, or construct or erect any building or structure of whatever kind whether permanent or temporary in character, or run or string any public service utility into, upon, or across such lands, except on special written permit and by authority of the Park Service." [Director, Park Service]

Q.—Who owns submerged lands?
Ownership of sovereignty submerged and tidal lands, including sandbars and banks, islands created by deposit of dredged soil, emergent

lands in the public waters and reclaimed sovereignty submerged or tidal lands, not heretofore conveyed by deed or statute, is vested in the Trustees of the Internal Improvement Fund of the State of Florida. The sovereignty submerged bottom lands of meandered fresh-water lakes vest in the State of Florida, subject to administrative jurisdiction of the Trustees of the Internal Improvement Fund. [Director, Trustees of the Internal Improvement Fund]

Q.—What is sovereignty land?
Sovereignty lands are those areas which vested in the State of Florida by the act of Congress approved March 3, 1845, which admitted Florida into the Union as a sovereign state. These sovereignty lands include the unsurveyed submerged bottom lands of meandered fresh-water lakes, the submerged and tidal lands in the coastal and intra-coastal waters, including natural sandbars and banks, islands created by deposits of spoil from dredging or other operations, submerged lands reclaimed by the lowering of the normal water level, and lands which emerged in the public waters within the territorial limits of the state. The boundary between sovereignty lands and public domain lands of upland or swamp and overflowed areas is the meander or surveyed line delineating the approximate line of mean high water and distinguishes the unsurveyed area classified as sovereignty from the areas surveyed as public domain lands. [Director, Trustees of the Internal Improvement Fund]

Q.—What public agency controls State-owned, submerged lands?
Title to the sovereignty submerged and tidal lands in and under the public coastal and intracoastal waters is vested in the Trustees of the Internal Improvement Fund (Section 253.12, Florida Statutes). [Director, Trustees of the Internal Improvement Fund]

Q.—What is "filled land"?
The term "filled land" generally designates areas which formerly were submerged or tidal lands in the public waters, and which areas have been raised to elevation above normal high water by the depositing of material upon the submerged or tidal area. [Director, Trustees of the Internal Improvement Fund]

Q.—How do I get a permit to fill the property in front of my bay house?
Permits to fill submerged or tidal lands in the public coastal and intracoastal waters may be granted by the local governing body to

the owner of the land, but such permit is conditional, requiring formal approval of the Trustees of the Internal Improvement Fund. Permit from the United States Army Corps of Engineers is also required. Establishment of a bulkhead line and ownership of the area proposed to be filled are prerequisites to the approval of a fill permit by the Trustees of the Internal Improvement Fund.

Objections to the issuance of a permit to fill submerged or tidal lands may be filed with the local governing body which issues such permit, with the United States Army Corps of Engineers and/or with the Trustees of the Internal Improvement Fund. Since the establishment of a bulkhead line generally is evidence that filling is contemplated, the logical time for protest against filling would be during the public hearing conducted by the local governing body in its proceedings to fix the location for its bulkhead lines. [Director, Trustees of the Internal Improvement Fund]

Q.—What are groynes?
Groynes are structures installed in the public waters marginal to upland for the purpose of deflecting water currents, stabilizing or protecting the shore or beach by arresting the drifting of sand and other material borne by water currents. [Director, Trustees of the Internal Improvement Fund]

Q.—I see frequent references in my newspaper to the "bulkhead line." What is a "bulkhead line"?
A bulkhead line is a legally established offshore line beyond which no sales of sovereignty submerged or tidal lands will be made by the Trustees of the Internal Improvement Fund into private ownership, nor private filling allowed. Bulkhead lines are fixed by the local governing body, subject to approval by the Trustees of the Internal Improvement Fund. [Director, Trustees of the Internal Improvement Fund]

Q.—Do I need a permit to search for treasure in long-wrecked ships?
State Lease or Permit is a prerequisite to any operation in the public coastal waters involving salvage of abandoned vessels, treasure, relics, or other materials in, on, or under the sovereignty submerged lands. (Section 253.03, Florida Statutes; *Massachusetts Co.* v. *State of Florida*, 95 So. 2nd 902.) In the interest of more effectively protecting and conserving relics, artifacts, and other materials of intrinsic value or historic interest, the processing of salvage leases and permits

has been suspended, pending adoption of new regulations. (It is quite possible that future authorizations for treasure and other salvage exploration will be limited to educational institutions and scientific and historical societies.) [Director, Trustees of the Internal Improvement Fund]

Q.—How far out to sea does the boundary of Florida extend?
The territorial boundary of Florida in the Atlantic Ocean, including the Straits of Florida, is three geographic miles seaward from the mean low water line of the coast in contact with the ocean. The boundary in the Gulf of Mexico has been established three marine leagues seaward from the mean low water line of land, but the location of the boundary for transition from the Atlantic Ocean in the vicinity of the Dry Tortugas to the three-league limit in the Gulf has not yet been defined. [Director, Trustees of the Internal Improvement Fund]

Q.—Can I buy pine seedlings from the Florida Forest Service?
Yes, you can buy pine seedlings from the Florida Forest Service. Time for application to buy is any time of the year. Time for delivery of seedlings to the purchaser is from about the middle of November to approximately March 1. Minimum order is 500 and the cost is $4.00 per thousand, F.O.B. Forest Service nurseries are at Munson, Olustee, Chiefland, and Punta Gorda.

Applications to purchase seedlings can be obtained from Farm Foresters and County Rangers, both of the Florida Forest Service, County Agents, Soil Conservation Service Offices, and of course the Florida Forest Service Headquarters.

Very few trees are more attractive than Florida's stately pine. In addition to their aesthetic value, they provide a real profit to the landowners. [State Forester]

Q.—What wild plants does Florida law seek to conserve?
The law provides penalties for the taking for sale or purchase, either from public land or without the owner's permission from private property, the following native Florida plants and trees (identified by scientific name in the statute): Dogwood, redbud or Judas tree, mountain laurel, trailing arbutus, dahoon, myrtleleaf, yaupon, and American holly; gopher wood (Torreya), Florida yew, royal palm, yellow jessamine, sweet bay, bromeliads, tillandsia (except Spanish moss), catopsis-Guzmania, and orchids.

Q.—How many national cemeteries are there in Florida?

There are two, the Barrancas National Cemetery at Pensacola and the St. Augustine National Cemetery at St. Augustine. Nineteen of the recovered casualties of the Battleship Maine originally buried in the Post Cemetery at the Key West Barracks, Key West, were subsequently disinterred and buried at the Arlington National Cemetery. Later, all other remains were removed from the Post Cemetery and reinterred in the Barrancas National Cemetery. [Chief, Cemetery Branch, Department of the Army]

Q.—How many State Parks are there in Florida?

The Florida Park Service regards twenty-eight of its parks as "operating," in the sense that these are either developed or partially developed. The Park Service also possesses the sites of eleven undeveloped parks. The Park Service has the additional responsibility of caring for twenty-three historic memorials. [Park Service]

Q.—Where can I get an air map of Florida?

Sectional air charts of Florida are available at most local airports at a cost of twenty-five cents each. The Florida Development Commission publishes an aviation directory giving considerable information about airports and seaplane bases in the state. A copy may be obtained by writing the Commission's Aviation Department at Tallahassee. [Development Commission]

Q.—What kinds of local service districts are there?

There are flood control, fire control, mosquito control, sanitary and storm sewer, drainage, lighting, library, hospital, airport, and perhaps other kinds of districts. They range in size from covering many counties to a few city blocks. Their purpose is to use the machinery of government to accomplish some special purpose desired by a majority of the people in that area. There are certainly hundreds, perhaps thousands, of these districts with legal life. Some are dormant, having outlived their usefulness. Others have been taken over by newer, larger districts with the same purpose.

Q.—How do local service districts operate?

It would be safe to say that nearly all, if not all, are financed by assessments which are shown on regular tax bills and become liens on the land if not paid. The assessments are limited, as a rule, to those lands benefiting from the district's services. Generally, they come into existence by a vote of the people in the proposed district. They are managed by boards (1) elected by the landowners, or (2) appointed by the Governor, or (3) selected by the Board of County Commissioners.

Q.—What is a flood control district?
As the name suggests, a flood control district serves the purpose of regulating the amount of water on land. The district may range in size from the Central and Southern Florida Flood Control District, covering all or part of seventeen counties, to local authorities with relatively few acres to protect. Originally, the drainage function— the removing of water from the land, usually by canals—was regarded as the purpose of such districts. Now, however, flood control has evolved into conservation. The water table is stabilized and maintained so that there is neither flood nor drought.

Q.—How many islands are there in the chain known as the Florida Keys?
A count of islands large enough to be shown on hydrographic maps of the United States Coast and Geodetic Survey totals 882. Map #1248, for Virginia Key and Biscayne Key, records 11 islands; Map #1249, Fowey Rock to Alligator Reef, 164; Map #1250, Alligator Reef to Sombrero Key, 242; Map #1251, Sombrero Key to Sand Key, 422; and Map #1252, Sand Key to Rebecca Shoal, 43. [State Geologist]

Q.—What is the meridian marker?
It is the spot from which all land in Florida is identified. This point of land is in Tallahassee, about four city blocks from the Capitol. Through this point run two invisible lines. The line running east and west is known as the base line. The line running north and south is known as the Tallahassee meridian. From that intersection, tiers of land known as townships are extended to cover the state. Each regular township is six miles square, and is numbered in the order of its proximity to Tallahassee. Each regular township is, in turn, divided into thirty-six sections, each section being one mile square. These sections are numbered in the same order everywhere, and each section is divided in an identical way.

Q.—How was the meridian marker located?
The Tallahassee principal meridian was established in 1824 by the United States Surveyor-General for Florida. He was directed to

begin the surveying of land in Florida from a point at the seat of government, Tallahassee.

This point of beginning was described as being "about a mile southwest from the deserted fields of Tallahassee, about a mile south of the Ocklocknee and Tallahassee trails at a point where the old Spanish road is intersected by a small trail running southwesterly." The point of intersection of the Tallahassee principal meridian and the parallel base line so established is at longitude 84° 16' 42" west from Greenwich and latitude 30° 28' north from the equator.

Q.—You speak of "invisible lines" crossing to form the marker. Is there something of "a physical nature" to be seen at this point?
Yes, there is a small monument over the point. This monument was placed in 1925. It may be seen in Tallahassee in the vicinity of Gaines and Calhoun streets, about a block to the south of the intersection of those main streets.

Taxes and Spending—
Homesteads and Exemptions

Q.—What taxes does a citizen of Florida pay?
A Floridian pays these taxes: (a) ad valorem taxes on real and tangible personal property (assessed and enforced by counties and municipalities of the State); (b) estate and inheritance taxes; (c) motor vehicle and drivers licenses; (d) motor fuel and gasoline taxes; (e) sales and use tax; (f) beverage tax; (g) cigaret tax; (h) racing tax; (i) intangible personal property tax; (j) 5 per cent wholesale excise tax on recreational or sporting goods (effective July 1, 1963); (k) utilities tax (1½ per cent). [Director, Revenue Commission]

Q.—What tax provides the most money?
The sales and use tax. [Director, Revenue Commission]

Q.—Is there a sales tax on everything?
No. Important exceptions include groceries, medicines, transportation tickets, and telephone and telegraph services.

Q.—Who gets the largest single share of the State's tax money?
Public schools receive around 64 per cent of the money disbursed through the General Revenue Fund.

Q.—Which is the second biggest user of tax money?
Highways. [Director, Revenue Commission]

Q.—What else does State tax money support?
Protection to persons and property; hospitals, health and sanitation; public welfare; institutions of higher learning; correctional institutions; general government; and aid to cities and counties. [Director, Revenue Commission]

Q.—What is tax "earmarking" and what taxes are earmarked for certain things?

When all or part of the money derived from a certain tax is committed to a specific use, the process is known as earmarking. Some economists deplore earmarking, contending that all tax proceeds should be paid into a pool from which the Legislature would appropriate. They feel the Legislature does not give the same scrutiny to earmarked money as it does to funds which must be reappropriated every other year. Legislators, however, seem to find it is easier to justify a new or additional tax by tying it directly to a public need. They think the taxpayer may feel better about paying the tax if he can say to himself, "Well, that'll bring better schools," or some other specific and accepted worthy purpose. Security buyers, too, like to have a proven source of revenue as the basis for repayment of their money. Florida in 1964, for instance, earned its best bond rating when securities were marketed that were tied to the utility gross receipts tax, a levy then with a 32-year record of productivity.

Among the taxes whose proceeds are committed either all or in part by constitutional or statutory earmarking are: gasoline tax, for highway construction and maintenance; sales tax, for schools; pari-mutuel wagering taxes, for counties; cigaret tax, collected within cities, for cities; wholesale tax on recreational and sporting goods, for land acquisition and recreational facilities.

Q.—What are State "trust funds"?

The State Treasury has many pockets. Revenue collected for a specific purpose is put into a separate pocket. It is being held in trust, to be spent only for the reason collected. For example, the tax on a box of citrus fruit is earmarked for advertising Florida citrus, so as to encourage its sale. Hence, the citrus advertising fund is a "trust fund."

Q.—What is the "General Revenue Fund"?

The day-to-day operations of the State government—the courts, universities, and prisons, for examples—are paid out of the State Treasury's biggest pocket. This is the one receiving the tax money not earmarked for any specific purpose. About one-half of the State's outgo is from the General Revenue Fund. There is another pocket known as the "Working Capital Fund," which consists only of any money left in the General Revenue Fund at the end of the two-year period, the biennium, for which the Legislature makes appropriations. Aside from the General Revenue Fund and the Working Capital Fund, all other money in the State Treasury belongs in trust funds for earmarked purposes.

Q.—Does Florida have a State income tax?
No. An income tax is prohibited under Article IX, Section 11, of the State Constitution. [Director, Revenue Commission]

Q.—Does Florida have an inheritance tax?
Yes. But it is limited to that portion for which the federal government allows credit on the federal return, and which, if not collected by the State, would go to the federal government anyway. [Director, Revenue Commission]

Q.—What is the intangible tax?
Intangible tax is against full cash value of intangible property such as stocks and shares, bonds (except bonds of municipalities or United States government), and bank deposits including money placed in savings and loan associations. [Director, Revenue Commission]

Q.—Is it true that Florida has a tax on rents now?
Florida's 3 per cent sales tax has applied to rents since enactment of the sales tax law in 1949. Until 1963 a tenant was exempt from this tax on rent after paying for six months. In 1963, however, the Legislature changed the time to one year.

Q.—What is the State fiscal year?
Florida's State fiscal year begins on July 1 and ends on June 30.

Q.—Who signs the State's checks?
The State government's checks are known as "warrants." A warrant is a written order for a payment from the State Treasury. It is prepared in the Office of the Comptroller, the officer who has the constitutional responsibility for determining that all charges against the State have been authorized by the Legislature and that there is sufficient money to pay a particular bill. The warrant is signed by the Governor and by the Comptroller. These signatures are applied mechanically. There have been instances when the Governor would direct the Comptroller not to sign his name to a specified warrant. Without the Governor's signature, the warrant could not be cashed by the State Treasurer.

Q.—Can counties or cities put on any taxes they please?
No. The Legislature controls the kind of taxes that cities and counties

can impose. While there are exceptions, the Legislature has tried to curb the imposition of taxes which duplicate those already imposed by the State. There is, for example, a direct prohibition against cities levying a sales tax. Cities share in the State's tax on cigarets and counties in the State's tax on gasoline. Otherwise, local government supports itself largely upon property taxation, occupational licenses, and franchise taxes.

Q.—What is the "full faith and credit" of the state?

The phrase "full faith and credit" is found in Article IV, Section 1, of the United States Constitution and is referred to as the "full faith and credit clause." In essence, the several states are required to give cognizance to the public acts, records, and judicial proceedings of another state in the same manner as would have been accorded such acts, records, and proceedings in such other state. Thus, a judgment entered in a court of a sister state having jurisdiction of the parties to the judgment is, under the federal Constitution, required to be accorded the same force and effect in the courts of other states. The word "faith" as appears in the subject clause signifies the acceptance by the recognizing state of the propriety of the proceedings in the sister state. The word "credit" in the subject clause signifies the accord given by the recognizing state to the acts of a sister state.

The phrase "full faith and credit" when put as in the question; that is, of the state, does not appear to have legal significance. Of late, the phrase has been quoted in news articles or contemporaneous speeches as denoting a moral obligation on the part of a state to repay monies borrowed by it from banking houses or bond holders, but such usage appears to be unrelated to the legal meaning of the phrase as found in the "full faith and credit clause" of the Constitution. [Attorney General]

Q.—When are property taxes due?

Taxes on real estate are payable to the County Tax Collector during November, with a 4 per cent discount from the face amount; during December with a 3 per cent discount; during January with a 2 per cent discount; during February with a 1 per cent discount; and during March at the face amount. The tax becomes delinquent on April 1.

Q.—What is a tax assessment?

It is the determining of the value of property for the purpose of taxation. If you own your home, it will be valued by the County Tax Assessor. This valuation becomes the basis for the tax bill. However, a very important element in figuring this bill is the rate of value used in your county. This varies widely from county to county. Because of the fixed amounts of the homestead tax exemption ($5,000) and the maximum school millage (20 mills), the rate of value materially affects the ultimate tax.

Q.—If I think the assessment on my property is wrong, do I have any way to appeal?

If a claim for exemption is rejected, the taxpayer has a right to appeal. The procedure is set forth in 31 Florida Jurisprudence, *Taxation*, Section 126, as follows: "If, after due consideration, the tax assessor finds that the applicant is not entitled to the exemption asked for he must give notice of disapproval with reasons, to enable the applicant, if he wishes, to make an appeal from the decision against him. The appeal is made to the Board of county commissioners sitting as a board of equalization, which may either reverse the decision and grant the exemption if it judges the applicant to be entitled to it or affirm the decision of the tax assessor. The action of the board is final unless the applicant within a prescribed period files in the circuit court of the county in which the homestead is situated a proceeding against the assessor for a declaratory decree or other appropriate proceeding. If the claimant is successful in the court proceeding, the decree will direct the assessor to grant the exemption." The procedure for appealing an assessment would be the same. [Attorney General]

Q.—What is "reassessment"?

The Attorney General says "reassessment can mean either the assessment of property for back taxes or a second assessment of property in a situation where the first assessment was improper." So much for the legal meaning. What most people likely think of when they chance across the word is something else—a change, usually upward, in the valuation of their homes or other property for tax purposes.

This problem really had its beginning prior to 1940 when the State levied a millage on real estate. Since the amount of money paid by the property owners in each county would depend upon the rate of local assessments, or valuations, there was a deliberate policy of driving these down. With a fixed statewide millage rate to be applied against local valuations, there was a dollars-and-cents advantage gained by property owners of a county having a rate of assessments lower than the rate in other counties.

Finally, the percentages of value—dropping as low in some counties as 25 or 30 per cent of cash worth—became so distorted and unproductive that the Legislature was able to abolish ad valorem taxation on real property for State purposes in 1940 without disrupting the tax economy.

But meantime a new element, the $5,000 homestead exemption, was brought into being in 1934. This hampered the restoring of assessments to real value after the State tax was abolished. To run the rate of assessments up would result in many owners of small residences having to pay taxes, or taxes in substantial amount, for the first time. For example, in a county assessing at 50 per cent of value, a $10,000 residence would be exempt from most taxation under the artificially inflated $5,000 exemption.

This under-valuation affected in two ways the problem of getting money necessary to run local governments, including schools. Owners of non-exempt property—rental residences and stores, for instance— had to pay more. And the local governments insisted upon participating in tax revenues collected by the State, either directly or indirectly. The Legislature, as a direct revenue source, gave the cities a share of the cigaret tax income collected within their boundaries. As an indirect source, the Legislature earmarked some sales tax revenue for schools.

But the pressure for bringing property assessments more in line with either "actual cash value" or "just value"—two of the legal terms used—continued. In a number of counties, the tax assessors— elected officials—sought to cushion the increase in rate by having professional assessment firms come in to appraise the current value of every piece of property. In other counties, the local assessors notched up the level of valuation. Each way was known popularly as "reassessment." Regardless of fairness and law, the word came to possess an ugly connotation for many owners of small homes. While millage rates were supposed to be proportionately reduced as assessment rates went up, obviously the real worth of the $5,000 homestead exemption was changed and reassessment resulted in some property owners paying county ad valorem taxes for the first time. Reassessments were matters of understandable political concern to local tax assessors.

Q.—What is homestead exemption?
There are two types of homestead exemption in Florida. Generally, people who speak of the "homestead exemption" are referring to the tax allowance. However, homesteads are also exempt from forced sale for the payment of certain kinds of debt.

Q.—Who can get homestead exemption?
As stated in Article X, Section 7, of the Florida Constitution, the homestead exemption is available to every person who has the legal title or beneficial title in equity to real property in this state and who resides thereon and in good faith makes the same his or her permanent home, or the permanent home of another or others legally or naturally dependent upon said person. [Attorney General]

Q.—How does the homestead tax exemption operate?
Florida's Constitution grants an exemption from taxation up to $5,000 of the assessed value of a home occupied either by the owner or by another "legally or naturally dependent" upon the owner. This exemption does not include assessments for special benefits, such as street paving. It should be noted that this exemption applies against the assessed value. The rate of property assessment for tax purposes varies from county to county, but the dollar value of the exemption likely will be more than $5,000.

Q.—Is it necessary to possess a Florida automobile tag to obtain homestead exemption?
No, the question of qualifying for homestead exemption is determined by the County Tax Assessor in other ways.

Q.—Do I have to vote in Florida in order to get homestead exemption?
It is not necessary to vote in Florida in order to claim homestead exemption. [Attorney General]

Q.—If I have two homes—say one in town and one at the beach— may I apply for homestead exemption on either one I choose?
The owner of two homes does not have an option to select which shall be entitled to homestead exemption. The home selected by the owner as a permanent place of residence is the one entitled to exemption, and whether it meets the statutory requirements must be determined as a question of fact, and not by choice of the owner. [Attorney General]

Q.—Can I rent my house for part of the year and still get homestead exemption?

Whether the owner of a house can rent the house and still get homestead exemption depends upon the particular circumstances of each case. Generally, a rental or lease of homestead premises is considered to be inconsistent with a claim for the tax exemption, and usually constitutes an abandonment of the homestead rights; however, a temporary renting may not waive the exemption right if there is an intent to return. Also, a rental of part of the homestead property constitutes an abandonment of a proportionate part of an exemption. [Attorney General]

Q.—What is the penalty for giving false information in claiming the homestead exemption?

A fine up to $500 and a jail sentence up to six months could be imposed.

Q.—How much land is regarded as a homestead?

For the purpose of this exemption, the size depends upon whether the homestead is inside an incorporated area—a city or town—or outside. Inside, a homestead may have a maximum size of a half-acre. Outside, the homestead may be 160 acres. In addition to the land and its improvements, the exemption applies also to personal property worth $1,000. This usually would be furniture.

Q.—What is the other homestead exemption?

The State Constitution safeguards family-owned property of Florida residents from sale by court order for judgments on debts not involving the homestead land and buildings. For example, a homestead may not be sold by a court to satisfy a judgment resulting from damages awarded as the result of an automobile accident. But the homestead can be sold if the owner fails to pay taxes and assessments, or if he does not make the agreed payments either on the purchase of the property or for the construction and repair of the structures on the land.

Q.—How else does the Constitution protect family property?

The Constitution requires both husband and wife to sign any document which would pledge the homestead. Neither the husband nor the wife alone may jeopardize the family's ownership of the homestead.

Q.—Do disabled persons get a special tax exemption?
Article IX, Section 9, of the Florida Constitution provides a special
exemption to every person who has lost a limb or been disabled in war
or by misfortune. Further exemptions are provided by Sections
192.11–192.113, Florida Statutes. [Attorney General]

Q.—How do you become a resident of Florida?
By this question you probably mean how do you become domiciled
in Florida. The Florida Supreme Court has said: "A legal residence
or domicile in this state may be acquired by one who, coming from
another state or country, actually lives in this state with the intention
of permanently remaining here. In such a case a domicile by choice
is established. Legal residence consists of fact and intention. Both
must concur." No particular length of time is necessary in order for a
person to establish his domicile in Florida. As soon as such person
is physically present in the state with the intention to remain here
permanently the state is his legal residence or domicile. [Comptroller]

Q.—Does Florida have legalized gambling?
The Legislature and the voters in the affected counties have authorized pari-mutuel wagering on horse and dog racing and jai alai
games.

*Q.—How much money does the state make off the race tracks and
frontons?*
The State Budget Director reported the yield from pari-mutuel
wagering establishments for the year ending June 30, 1964, was
$32,815,543.

Q.—Who can get a license to sell beer?
The personal requirements for an applicant to obtain a beer license
in Florida are provided in Section 561.15, Florida Statutes. These
are that the person must be of good moral character and not less than
twenty-one years of age, and must not have been convicted within
the last five years of any offense against the beverage laws of Florida,
the United States, or any other state, and must not have been convicted within the last past five years in Florida, any other state, or the
United States, of soliciting for prostitution, pandering, letting premises for prostitution, keeping a disorderly place, or illegally dealing in
narcotics, and must not have been convicted in the last past fifteen
years of any felony in Florida, any other state, or the United States.

There is no limitation on the number of beer licenses that can be issued. [Resident Attorney, Beverage Department]

Q.—How can I get a license to sell whiskey?
The same personal requirements apply to applicants for liquor licenses in Florida and, in addition, the quota of liquor licenses is one for every 2,500 inhabitants in an incorporated municipality or in the territory of any county lying outside of such municipalities according to the last regular statewide census. This quota limitation on liquor licenses is contained in Subsection (1) of Section 561.20, Florida Statutes. [Resident Attorney, Beverage Department]

Q.—Could I make wine for my own use?
Floridians cannot legally make wine for their own use unless they obtain a license to manufacture wine. The annual cost of such a license is $100 as provided in Section 561.35, Florida Statutes. [Resident Attorney, Beverage Department]

Q.—Is it possible to set up a distillery in Florida? In a dry county?
It is possible to start a distillery in Florida to make alcohol for beverages or other sale. The annual license fee as provided in Section 561.35, Florida Statutes, is $1,500. Under the provisions of Section 561.43, Florida Statutes, such a distillery can be located in a dry county but its products can only be sold for transportation out of the county. In fact, the only distillery in Florida has been located for many years in Polk County which was a dry county until 1963. [Resident Attorney, Beverage Department]

Q.—What is a dry county, and how many of these are there?
A dry county is one in which only beverages containing not more than 3.2 per cent of alcohol by weight may be sold. As of 1964, these were the dry counties: Bradford, Calhoun, Clay, Gadsden, Hamilton, Hardee, Holmes, Jackson, Jefferson, Lafayette, Liberty, Madison, Santa Rosa, Suwannee, Walton, Washington, and Wakulla.

Q.—Has any specific State tax ever been lowered?
Yes. An example could be the tax on intangibles, which was reduced from two mills on the dollar to one and a half mills in 1963 and then to one mill in 1964.

Q.—Has any specific State tax ever been abolished?
Yes. An important source of State revenue for many years was the ad valorem taxation of real and personal property, for example, land and buildings. This tax was abolished in 1940.

Motoring—Tags and Licenses

*Q.—How soon must a new resident get a Florida automobile license
tag?*
The law makes no provision for a grace period. The Florida tag must
be obtained just as soon as the newcomer is either gainfully employed
or enrolls children in the public schools.

Q.—Where do I get an automobile license?
From the office of the County Tax Collector in your county or from
the Motor Vehicle Commissioner, Tallahassee.

Q.—What determines the cost of a motor vehicle license tag?
The fee is based upon the weight and type of the vehicle. For the
automobile in family use, the requirements may be determined from
the letter appearing on its tag (or from the absence of a letter).
Automobiles weighing up to 2,500 pounds (and in private use) take
a "D" tag. Automobiles weighing more than 2,500 pounds but not
more than 3,500 require a "plain" license, or one without an identifying letter. Automobiles weighing more than 3,500 but not more
than 4,500 carry a "W" tag. Automobiles weighing more than 4,500
take a "WW" tag. The fee is subject to change from time to time
by the Legislature. In Florida, the annual tag is the only tax paid
(other than the sales tax at the time of purchase) on the automobile.
It is exempt from the property tax levied in many states.

*Q.—Does the price of an automobile license vary from county to
county?*
No, the rates apply uniformly statewide.

Q.—When is the deadline for getting an automobile license?
The 20th day of the month following the beginning of sale. Because
of a staggering arrangement, by which the start of the annual sale is

being moved from January 1 to July 1, the deadline will change each year until 1970. The Governor may, at his discretion, extend the deadline by 30 days whenever an emergency exists. Such an emergency might be a crop failure which would cause economic distress to many tag purchasers.

Q.—Where does the money from the sale of auto tags go?
Approximately 35 per cent of the tag revenue goes into local school construction; the balance into the State's General Revenue Fund for the support of government generally.

Q.—Who may buy a tag with a 68 number?
Anyone purchasing a tag from the Motor Vehicle Commissioner at Tallahassee. The numbers 1 through 67 stand for the counties of issuance.

Q.—How do the counties get their identifying numbers on license tags?
The numbers are based upon the tags sold in 1937. Dade County, having the largest sale that year, drew the prefix "1" and Liberty County, with the smallest sale, "67." While counties have shifted position in the rank of sale, the county-designating numerals remain as originally established, in part as a convenience to law enforcement authorities.

Q.—Can tags be bought for parts of a year?
Yes, half-year and quarter-year tags may be purchased for automobiles being registered in Florida for the first time. A monthly pro-rata basis is provided for the registration of trucks and trailers (other than house trailers).

Q.—Where can I get a driver's license?
Enquire at any Florida Highway Patrol Station for its examining schedule. [Director, Department of Public Safety]

Q.—Must new residents wait until their birth month to get a new license?
No. Every newcomer should obtain his Florida license immediately. [Director, Department of Public Safety]

Q.—How much will a driver's license cost?
An operator's license is $3.00, a chauffeur's, $5.00. These licenses are normally good for two years. [Director, Department of Public Safety]

Q.—When do driver's licenses expire in Florida?
The last day of the licensee's birth month, two years after purchase of the license. [Director, Department of Public Safety]

Q.—Can new residents with an out-of-state driver's license get a Florida license without taking an examination?
No. Every newcomer must take the vision and written examinations, but those with valid licenses from other states are not required to take the driving test. [Director, Department of Public Safety]

Q.—Is there any way to prepare for the driving test?
Every applicant should study the *Florida Driver's Handbook,* available at all Highway Patrol Stations. [Director, Department of Public Safety]

Q.—How many times can I take the driver's license test?
Five times; it may then be retaken after a waiting period. [Director, Department of Public Safety]

Q.—Does Florida have automatic re-examination of driving skills?
No. [Director, Department of Public Safety]

Q.—How old must I be to get a driver's license in Florida?
The minimum age is sixteen, except for a restricted operator's, which is fourteen. [Director, Department of Public Safety]

Q.—Does Florida participate in the national clearing house of drivers who have lost their licenses?
Yes, Florida exchanges information on driver licensing and revocation.

Q.—Is a bicycle license required in Florida?
The State does not require a license for bicycles. Some cities do.

Q.—How much does a license for a house trailer cost in Florida?
A house trailer license plate in Florida costs $16.25 plus a 50-cent service fee. [Motor Vehicle Commissioner]

Q.—Do I need a motor vehicle license for an airplane in Florida?
Aircraft owned by residents of this state must be registered each year; such aircraft registration is handled by the County Tax Collector's office or by the Motor Vehicle Commission. [Motor Vehicle Commissioner]

Health and Welfare—Marriages,
Divorces, Mental Health

Q.—Where do I get a marriage license?
At the Office of the County Judge.

Q.—What requirements does one have to meet to get a marriage license?
Applicants for a marriage license must be at least twenty-one years old or file with the County Judge the written consent of parents. The actual issuance of the license may not take place until three days from the day of application. During the three-day period the application for license must be posted at the front door of the courthouse. Every person applying for a marriage license must file a certificate from a physician stating that the applicant has been given a physical examination including a blood test for the discovery of venereal disease. It is required that this examination be done within thirty days of the date of application for the marriage license.

Q.—How much does a marriage license cost?
The cost is $3.50.

Q.—What are grounds for divorce in Florida?
The grounds for divorce are listed in Section 65.04, Florida Statutes, as follows: "No divorce shall be granted unless one of the following facts shall appear:
(1) That the parties are within the degrees prohibited by law.
(2) That the defendant is naturally impotent.
(3) That the defendant has been guilty of adultery.
If it shall appear to the court that the adultery complained of was occasioned by collusion of the parties, and done with the intent to

procure a divorce, or that both parties have been guilty of adultery, no divorce shall be decreed.

(4) Extreme cruelty by defendant to complainant.

(5) Habitual indulgence by defendant in violent and ungovernable temper.

(6) Habitual intemperance of defendant or habitual use of narcotics by defendant.

(7) Willful, obstinate and continued desertion of complainant by defendant for one year.

(8) That the defendant has obtained a divorce from the complainant in any other state or country.

(9) That either party had a husband or wife living at the time of the marriage sought to be annulled."
[Attorney General]

Q.—Can you get a "quickie" divorce in Florida?

Chapter 65, Florida Statutes, provides that in order to obtain a divorce in Florida, the complainant must have resided six months in the state before filing a complaint for divorce. The prescription of such six-months residency period appears to be a manifestation of legislative intent to prevent Florida from becoming a mecca for those seeking instant release from the bonds of matrimony. It is notable that in 1957 the residency requirements were increased from ninety days to six months. The length of the residency requirement varies from state to state and being a creation of legislative action is subject to change from time to time, as occurred in 1957 with our law.
[Attorney General]

Q.—Where are records of births, deaths, marriages, and divorces kept?

All birth and death records are filed at the Bureau of Vital Statistics, State Board of Health, Jacksonville, Florida.

Marriage and divorce records since June, 1927, are also maintained in the Bureau of Vital Statistics at Jacksonville. Each County Judge has records of every marriage when the marriage certificate was obtained in his county. This includes marriages both prior to June, 1927, and subsequent to June, 1927.

The Clerk of the Circuit Court has records of all divorces granted in his county, including those granted prior to June, 1927, and subsequent to June, 1927. [State Health Officer]

Q.—How may a person get a birth certificate?
A person born in Florida may obtain a birth certificate by applying to the Bureau of Vital Statistics, Florida State Board of Health, P. O. Box 210, Jacksonville, Florida. The fee is $1.00 for each certified copy or birth registration card. The certified copy is a picture of the original certificate. The birth registration card is wallet-sized and sealed in plastic. It shows the person's name, date and place of birth, birth certificate number, race, and sex. When the exact date of birth is unknown and more than one year of records is to be searched, the fee is $1.00 for each year searched up to a maximum of $25.00. In order for a thorough search to be made, the applicant should furnish his name at birth, date and place of birth, father's name, mother's maiden name, sex, and race. [State Health Officer]

Q.—How old are Florida's birth records?
The first State law requiring registration of births was enacted in 1899; however, there are some birth records on file dating back to 1865. [State Health Officer]

Q.—How can a birth certificate be obtained where no record exists?
In the case of births occurring prior to official records, or if a search indicates that there is no certificate on file, instructions and forms for filing a delayed birth certificate will be sent to the applicant. It is then up to the applicant to furnish documentary evidence proving the date and place of birth so that a certificate may be placed on file. The fee for filing a delayed birth certificate is $5.00. [State Health Officer]

Q.—How does a person get admitted to, or released from, a State mental hospital?
There are a number of procedures under which patients may be admitted to our State hospitals. Patients are received on commitment by the County Courts, the Circuit Courts, the Courts of Record, and the Criminal Courts of Record; on Order of Certification by the County Judge; on voluntary admission; on transfers from other state hospitals and on return from trial visit.

Commitments through the courts mentioned are for an indefinite period, as distinguished from the Order of Certification procedure which, being intended for those whose illness would appear to be relatively brief in duration, is limited to not more than six months.

If hospitalization beyond this six-months period is needed, then regular commitment is required.

I might mention that only those who have been bona fide residents of the State of Florida for a period of at least one year immediately prior to commitment are eligible for care and treatment in our State hospitals. In those instances where it becomes necessary for a County Judge to commit a non-resident patient, he is accepted for admission on a temporary basis until such time as arrangements can be completed for transfer of the patient to his state of legal residence.

The voluntary admission procedure is designed to provide hospitalization and treatment for those who, being aware that they are in need of psychiatric treatment, voluntarily request admission to the hospital and agree to fully cooperate with the hospital in the treatment program. This type admission does not involve any court proceedings and the patient may voluntarily leave the hospital at his own request on 24-hour notice. Those contemplating voluntary admission should first consult with a physician or psychiatrist in their home area to determine whether it might be advisable for the patient to visit the hospital and seek voluntary admission and, if so, have the physician arrange an appointment at the hospital for the patient.

There are also several methods of releasing patients, the principal types of releases being by trial visit and by competency discharge.

Trial visit contemplates the release of a patient under supervision of a responsible relative who assumes care of the patient in the home during a trial period of readjustment outside the hospital. Under this release, which customarily lasts for one year, the patient may be returned to the hospital for further treatment if needed. If the patient makes satisfactory adjustment and remains absent from the hospital for one year, he is automatically discharged.

Release by competency discharge is granted when, in the opinion of the hospital staff, the patient has regained competency and no longer requires hospitalization or supervision. Under this discharge the original certificate of competency is forwarded by the hospital to the committing court, and in absence of protest by the State Attorney within 20 days, the patient's judicial sanity is automatically restored. Patients who have court charges pending against them may be released only on discharge and then must be returned to the court of jurisdiction.

Other releases include discharges of non-residents for the purpose of transfer to their respective states of residence and discharges for transfer of veterans to Veterans Administration Hospitals when acceptable and authorized. [Director, Division of Mental Health]

Q.—How can a person get admitted to the Alcoholic Rehabilitation Center at Avon Park?

Only by being referred by medical doctors or osteopathic physicians licensed in this state, or by one of the Center's out-patient clinics. Patients are received only on a voluntary basis. No one can be committed to the Center for treatment. A patient is admitted by appointment, being notified when a bed will become available. Admission is on a first-come, first-served rotation. Patients must be bona fide residents of this state for at least one year immediately prior to making application for admission. Patients cannot be accepted who have court action pending or are on furlough from a State hospital.

Q.—Where are the Alcoholic Rehabilitation Center's out-patient clinics?

In Jacksonville, at 1241 S. McDuff Avenue; Miami, 1637 N. W. 10th Avenue; Pensacola, 1107 W. Avery Street; Tampa, Room 206, Professional Arts Building, 420 West Kennedy Street; and Orlando, 2603 N. Orange Avenue. See listing under State of Florida offices for telephone numbers.

Q.—How much does treatment cost at the Avon Park Alcoholic Rehabilitation Center? And the out-patient clinics?

At the Center, $12.50 per patient day; at the clinics, from nothing up to $8.50, depending upon individual circumstances. No otherwise eligible person can be refused treatment either at the Center or clinics by reason of inability to pay.

Q.—Can anyone get free shots at the County Health Departments?

While the availability of immunization varies from county to county, the answer in general is no. Free shots are usually reserved for the indigent and low-income groups. [State Health Officer]

Q.—Do all counties have mental health clinics?

Not all counties have mental health clinics because these require rather specialized personnel which would not be available in the smaller counties. There is, however, a mental health program in every county carried on by the Health Officer and nursing staff, and in most of the counties a mental health worker. [State Health Officer]

Q.—Must a State agency approve adoptions of children in Florida?
Approval of adoptions of children in Florida is a judicial function.
The Department of Public Welfare, as well as private agencies, may
make recommendations to the court with regard to the financial
ability and suitability of prospective adoptive parents. Approval,
however, must be made by the judge. [Director, Department of Public Welfare]

Q.—What does ADC mean?
ADC means the assistance program formerly known as Aid to Dependent Children. In 1962 Congress changed the name of this program to Aid and Services to Needy Families with Children. The
short title used for this program is Aid to Families with Dependent
Children (AFDC). [Director, Department of Public Welfare]

*Q.—Can a penniless elderly man or woman move to Florida and get
    old age assistance?*
A penniless elderly man or woman moving to Florida cannot receive
old age assistance until they have met the residency requirement.
Under the State Welfare Act a person to be eligible for assistance
must have resided in Florida for five years out of the last nine and
one year immediately prior to making application. This, incidentally,
is the maximum residence which it is possible to require and still
receive federal matching funds under the Social Security Act. Under
Medical Assistance for the Aged, however, a person merely needs to
establish proof that he is a resident of Florida to become eligible for
benefits. [Director, Department of Public Welfare]

*Q.—What sort of medical care to the aged does the State of Florida
    provide?*
The aged in Florida, under programs administered by the Department of Public Welfare, receive medical care as two different groups
of people. Persons eligible to receive a money grant under Medical
Assistance for the Aged are also eligible for hospital care for acute
illness, injury, or for cancer, for a period of 30 days during a 12-
month period, for medicines prescribed by a licensed physician, and
for nursing care at a nursing home. These same benefits are provided
for recipients of Aid to the Blind and of Aid to the Permanently and
Totally Disabled. Under the Aid to Families with Dependent Children Program hospital care only is provided.

The second group of aged are those qualifying under the Medical

Assistance for the Aged Program. Under this program a person over sixty-five who cannot pay the cost of medical care may be eligible to receive hospital care for acute illness, injury, or cancer, for a period of thirty days in a twelve-month period. An eligible person may, at any time, be provided home nursing care prescribed by a physician for either acute or chronic illness. Payments are made direct to the visiting nurse organization. No other benefits are available under this program. [Director, Department of Public Welfare]

Q.—What is meant by the phrase "welfare rolls"?
The 1951 State Legislature used the phrase "welfare rolls" when amending the State Welfare Act, Chapter 409, to require the Department of Public Welfare to furnish quarterly to the Clerk of the Circuit Court in every county a list showing the name, address, and amount of financial assistance received by recipients of public welfare. Internally, these lists are known as "assistance rolls" since the financial grant is based on need under requirement of the federal Social Security Act. [Director, Department of Public Welfare]

Q.—How soon can I get unemployment compensation in Florida?
It is assumed that the question relates only to Florida law, and does not involve benefit rights based on employment in other states, for which claims can be filed in Florida against such states at any time.

Nine months would be about the shortest possible time in which a worker could accumulate qualifying wages in Florida and, if otherwise eligible, receive his first benefit check based on those wages.

He must have been paid wages for insured work equal to twenty times his average weekly wages during his base period, and the law provides a "lag" period of one calendar quarter in which his initial claim is filed. When there are no delaying circumstances, such as need for further information to clarify or complete the claim, the normal interval between filing of the initial claim and receipt of the first benefit check is three weeks. [Chairman, Florida Industrial Commission]

Q.—Do I have to notify the Social Security Office if I move to Florida?
Only those persons receiving monthly Social Security benefit checks need to notify the Social Security Office if they move. The post office at home should also be asked to forward to the Florida address any benefit check received before the Social Security Administration

has made the address change effective. [District Manager, Social Security Administration]

Q.—Can I have the water from my well tested by the State Health Department?
Although the State Health Department does not generally perform chemical analyses on private water supplies, it does offer the service for bacteriological testing to determine potability of the water. This service can usually be obtained by contacting the County Health Department, such local Health Department office being at the county seat. [State Health Officer]

Q.—Do I have to have a special permit to build a swimming pool?
The State Health Department does not have statewide regulations on so-called private or backyard pools, which are defined in the Florida Sanitary Code: "(4) 'Private pool, bath house, or bathing place'— a facility used only by an individual citizen and his family or house guests and shall not include any type of cooperative housing or joint tenancy of three or more families." Some municipalities have regulations on private pools, and, therefore, local authorities should be consulted.

There are regulations of the State Board of Health on public pools, and approval of the plans and specifications, required to be prepared by a registered Florida engineer, must be obtained before commencing construction. Public pools include those operated by or at hotels, motels, tourist courts, apartment houses, clubs, schools, or institutions for patrons, members, or students. [State Health Officer]

Q.—Who supervises nursing homes? Who supervises trailer parks?
Nursing homes and trailer parks are supervised by the Florida State Board of Health. [State Health Officer]

Hunting and Fresh-Water Fishing

Q.—Where can I get a hunting license?
Hunting licenses may be purchased from any County Judge or his agent. [Director, Game and Fresh Water Fish Commission]

Q.—Where can I find out the exact dates each year for hunting season?
Dates are shown on the Hunting Summary available from the Game and Fresh Water Fish Commission or any County Judge. [Director, Game and Fresh Water Fish Commission]

Q.—What license is required to hunt in Florida and how much does it cost?
The following is a list and explanation of hunting and trapping licenses issued in Florida. Except as where indicated, licenses are issued from the Office of the County Judge in each county. Costs include the County Judge's fee. State residents sixty-five years and over and all children are exempt. Personnel of the military services stationed in Florida are considered residents of Florida insofar as licenses to hunt and fish are concerned.

GAME

Series H —For hunting on licensed private hunting preserves only ....$ 5.50

Series I —Resident, County 2.00

Series J —Resident, other than Home County.................. 4.50

Series K —Resident, State 7.50

Series L —Non-Resident, State 26.50

Series M —Non-Resident, 10 day Continuous 11.50

Series M-1—Non-Resident, County, for persons owning and paying taxes on 3,000 acres of land in the state, valid only in the county where the land occurs 11.50

Series Y—Guide, required for guiding hunting parties. Issued from office of Commission, Tallahassee 10.00

Alien Hunting—Issued from office of Commission,
Tallahassee 50.00

TRAPPING

Series N—Resident, County ....$ 3.25

Series O—Non-Resident, County 25.50

Series P—Resident, State 25.50

Series Q—Resident, other than Home County 10.50

Series R—Non-Resident, State 100.50

[Director, Game and Fresh Water Fish Commission]

Q.—Does the State maintain public hunting areas?
The State has 29 Wildlife Management Areas totaling nearly 4 million acres. [Director, Game and Fresh Water Fish Commission]

Q.—Do you need a special permit to hunt on the State hunting grounds?
A Public Hunt Permit is required to hunt on Wildlife Management Areas. [Director, Game and Fresh Water Fish Commission]

Q.—What birds are protected at all times by Florida law?
All birds, other than game birds during open season and crows, starlings, vultures, and English sparrows, are protected at all times and may not be hunted. Game birds are: quail, turkey, mourning doves, ducks, geese, rails and gallinules, coot, snipe, woodcock, and gallinaceous species such as pheasant now undergoing experimental release in the state. [Director, Game and Fresh Water Fish Commission]

Q.—Can anyone hunt alligators?
There is no open season on alligators in Florida. [Director, Game and Fresh Water Fish Commission]

Q.—Why are alligators protected?
Alligators are a valuable resource to Florida for their scenic value. In addition, they perform a useful service, in dry periods, by digging water holes valuable to other wildlife and fish. In the Everglades, for example, the water in 'gator holes may be the only open water for miles. This water is used for drinking by terrestrial animals and in it may live a nucleus of aquatic forms until the next rainy season. [Director, Game and Fresh Water Fish Commission]

Q.—Do I have to have a permit for a gun used only for hunting?
No, except for pistols. [Director, Game and Fresh Water Fish Commission]

Q.—How can I get a gun permit in Florida?
Permits for pistols or repeating rifles are issued by the various Boards of County Commissioners. [Director, Game and Fresh Water Fish Commission]

Q.—Can rabbits be hunted year-round?
There is no closed season on rabbits and they may be hunted throughout the year. [Director, Game and Fresh Water Fish Commission]

Q.—What animals may be hunted year-round?
There is no closed season on rabbits, skunks, opossums, foxes, bobcats, raccoons, armadillos, crows, starlings, vultures, and English sparrows. [Director, Game and Fresh Water Fish Commission]

Q.—Can I hunt anywhere in Florida?
Hunting by properly licensed hunters is permitted throughout the state during open season on lands not posted against hunting by the owner or not closed to hunting by a State or federal agency. [Director, Game and Fresh Water Fish Commission]

Q.—Who regulates fresh-water fishing?
Florida Game and Fresh Water Fish Commission. [Director, Game and Fresh Water Fish Commission]

Q.—Can I fish in any lake or pond or river I please?
Yes. In some instances permission must be obtained from landowners to go upon private ponds; also, some areas are closed to fishing by regulations or law. [Director, Game and Fresh Water Fish Commission]

Q.—What about out-of-state visitors—do they have to get fresh-water fishing licenses?
All non-residents except children under fifteen years of age must buy non-resident licenses to take fresh-water fish by any method. [Director, Game and Fresh Water Fish Commission]

Q.—Is there a closed season on fresh-water fish?
No. [Director, Game and Fresh Water Fish Commission]

Q.—Is there a bag limit on fresh-water fish?
Yes. Daily bag limit: 10 black bass, 15 pickerel, 30 white bass, 35

pan fish (bream, perch, and red finned pike); total of 90 in aggregate. Total possession limit: two days' bag limit after first day of fishing. [Director, Game and Fresh Water Fish Commission]

Q.—Do I need a license for fresh-water fishing?
All residents of Florida from fifteen to sixty-five years of age must possess a valid fishing license to take fresh-water fish; except that a license is not required of residents to fish noncommercially with not more than 3 poles in the county of their legal residence, except on fish management areas duly established by action of the Game and Fresh Water Fish Commission and the Board of County Commissioners of the area affected. The county resident exemption does not apply on these fish management areas. [Director, Game and Fresh Water Fish Commission]

Q.—Can I sell any fresh-water fish I catch?
No, unless you have a fish dealer's license, in which event you can sell nongame fish, specifically, catfish, suckers, etc. [Director, Game and Fresh Water Fish Commission]

Q.—Does the State regulate the fishing camp operators?
The State does not regulate fish camp operators as such, although they must have licenses to rent boats or to sell fresh-water fish (nongame). [Director, Game and Fresh Water Fish Commission]

Q.—Can I buy fish from a State hatchery?
No. The fish are free if the pond to be stocked meets specifications and if management procedures are followed. Largemouth bass and bluegill are available from the Florida Game and Fresh Water Fish Commission or the United States Fish and Wildlife Service, the agency of the federal government having jurisdiction over fish and wildlife. [Chief, Fisheries Division, Game and Fresh Water Fish Commission]

Q.—What does the money from fresh-water fishing licenses go for?
Into the State Game Fund, to be used by the Commission to carry out its duties. [Director, Game and Fresh Water Fish Commission]

Pleasure Boating,
Salt-Water Fishing

Q.—Do I have to register a boat in Florida?

Boats propelled by machinery in excess of 10 horsepower must be registered, except documented vessels, racing hulls, those used exclusively on private lakes, those owned by the United States, and ships' lifeboats. [Director, Board of Conservation]

Q.—How do I register a boat?

Pleasure-boat owners should apply for registration to the Tax Collector of the county in which a vessel is domiciled. Commercial boats are registered with the State Board of Conservation or with the Game and Fresh Water Fish Commission, depending on whether they operate in salt or fresh water. [Director, Board of Conservation]

Q.—Can I launch my boat anywhere I find a ramp?

Yes, if the ramps are public ramps. There are numerous privately owned ramps which charge a fee for launching. [Director, Board of Conservation]

Q.—Must a boat trailer have a license?

An automobile trailer used for transporting boats must be licensed as any other trailer hauled by an automobile. The licenses are issued by the Motor Vehicle Commissioner, generally through the County Tax Collectors as the Commissioner's agents. In addition to a license, boat trailers must be equipped with a combination tail-brake-tag light and directional turn lights. [Director, Board of Conservation]

Q.—Can a visitor bring in a boat from out of state and use it?

Yes. An out-of-state boat, if properly registered in its home state, may use Florida waters for a period of ninety days. [Director, Board of Conservation]

Q.—Do law enforcement officers enforce "traffic" laws on the water?
Yes. The water "rules of the road" are a part of the safety code, and
violation of the rules makes the boat operator liable to arrest for
recklessness. [Director, Board of Conservation]

Q.—What safety equipment must I have?
Required safety equipment varies with the size of the boat, but all
craft must carry one Coast-Guard-approved lifesaving device for
each person aboard, a white light visible for at least one mile and
capable of shining its beam all around the horizon, and an anchor
with appropriate rope. [Director, Board of Conservation]

Q.—How much tax will I have to pay on my boat?
The registration tax ranges from $1 for motorboats less than 12 feet
in length to $75 for those 110 feet or more in length. There is no
tangible personal property tax levied against boats. [Director, Board
of Conservation]

Q.—Where does the tax money on boats go?
The revenue from the registration certificate tax is distributed among
the various counties on the basis of number of boats registered in each
county. However, $2.50 of each registration fee for boats 12 feet or
more in length goes to the State for administration and enforcement
of the registration law. Any surplus in the State's share goes into the
Outdoor Recreation Land Acquisition Trust Fund. [Director, Board
of Conservation]

Q.—Is it possible to lose a boating license as it is to lose a driver's
     license?
There is no provision in Florida law for suspension or revocation of a
motorboat registration certificate. [Director, Board of Conservation]

Q.—Does the State regulate privately owned marinas?
No. [Director, Board of Conservation]

Q.—Does the State maintain any marinas?
No, with one exception. The Development Commission's Marine
Welcome Station at Fernandina Beach has a marina that is main-
tained by the Commission. [Director, Board of Conservation]

Q.—Where can I get a chart of any area of the Florida coastal
     waters?
From the director, Coast and Geodetic Survey, United States De-

partment of Commerce, Washington, D. C. In addition, most marinas and marine hardware stores have marine charts available at nominal cost. [Director, Board of Conservation]

Q.—Can a boatowner join the Coast Guard Auxiliary?
Yes. [Director, Board of Conservation]

Q.—Does the State regulate commercial fishing?
Yes; by law both general and local, and by rules adopted by the Board of Conservation. [Director, Board of Conservation]

Q.—Who regulates salt-water fishing in Florida?
Salt Water Fisheries Division, Board of Conservation. [Director, Board of Conservation]

Q.—Do I need a license for salt-water fishing?
No. [Director, Board of Conservation]

Q.—Can I sell any salt-water fish I catch?
If you are a Florida resident you may sell salt-water fish to a licensed wholesale dealer without obtaining a license yourself. If you sell directly to consumer you must have a retail dealer's license ($10 a year). A non-resident must obtain a non-resident commercial fisherman's license to sell his fish ($25). [Director, Board of Conservation]

Q.—Does the State regulate salt-water fishing guides and party boats?
Salt-water fishing guides and party boat operators must have a commercial registration (license) for their boats. The United States Coast Guard regulates boat operators who carry persons for hire. [Director, Board of Conservation]

Q.—Are there any bag limits on salt-water fish?
Yes. Snook, 4 daily; tarpon, unlawful to possess more than 2; sailfish, unlawful to possess more than 2; striped bass, unlawful to possess more than 6; shad, 15 daily taken by hook and line only. It is unlawful to possess more than a 2-day bag limit (8) of snook. In Bay County only there is a limit of 35 daily on speckled trout (weakfish). [Director, Board of Conservation]

Q.—Are there any closed seasons on salt-water fish?
There is no closed season on fin fish; but there are closed seasons on crawfish (March 31 to August 1), stone crabs (June 1 to October 15), and oysters (May 1 to September 1). There are minimum legal lengths on fin fish: 10 inches for bluefish and pompano (9 inches in

Lee County), 11 inches on flounder, and 12 inches on mackerel, redfish, speckled trout (weakfish), and lisa (black mullet). Lisa may be 10 inches west of the Aucilla River to the Alabama line, and 11 inches from the Aucilla to the Withlacoochee River. There is no size limit on trout in Wakulla, Gulf, and Bay counties. [Director, Board of Conservation]

Q.—How does the State distinguish between sport fish, game fish, and food fish?
Game fish are defined by law—snook, sailfish, tarpon, and striped bass. Many food fish such as snapper, mackerel, grouper, etc., are also highly regarded by sportsmen as sport fish. State law makes no distinction between "sport fish" and "game fish." Many pleasure fishermen regard sport fish as the big fellows like sailfish, marlin, and tuna but this, of course, is a matter of individual opinion. [Director, Board of Conservation]

Q.—Can anybody legally catch mullet with a net?
Yes, but only in those areas where netting is permitted. However, the use of hand nets operated by one person (cast nets) are lawful almost universally. [Director, Board of Conservation]

Q.—Why did the Board of Conservation change the name of mullet to lisa?
Lisa is Spanish for black mullet. The name was changed in a move to increase marketability of the fish. Several trash fish in the north are known as mullet, and many northern visitors look upon black mullet as only a bait fish. [Director, Board of Conservation]

Q.—Are there any laws about scuba diving?
There are no laws regulating scuba diving as such. [Director, Board of Conservation]

Q.—Is spear fishing legal in Florida?
Several counties have restrictions against spear fishing by local law. Prospective spear fishermen should contact local conservation officers. [Director, Board of Conservation]

Q.—What is "red tide"?
"Red tide" is a popular name given to discolored waters caused by the aggregation or tremendous increase (blooming) of microscopic organisms. This name was evidently coined for the phenomenon occurring along the west coast of Florida wherein a species of dino-

flagellate, *Gymnodinium brevis* Davis, periodically "bloomed," discolored the water, and resulted in "fish kills." The term is now used for nearly all biological phenomena resulting in the discoloration of waters even if "fish kills" do not occur. In a number of cases since 1946, "blooms" of *G. brevis* have been associated with catastrophic mass mortality of marine organisms. [Director, Board of Conservation]

Q.—What is the state doing about Jim Brevis, the red tide?
The State Conservation Department began intensive research in 1947. During much of this time, the United States Bureau of Commercial Fisheries also has been heavily committed to this investigation. Much is known about "Jim Brevis," as the red tide is popularly known, but the studies have yet to discover a weak link in the germinative process which might bring about its control. [Director, Board of Conservation]

Q.—If it's not a closed season on oysters, may I wade out in shallow bay waters and pick up all I want?
Yes, providing they are of the minimum legal size of 3 inches in diameter. [Director, Board of Conservation]

Roads and Bridges

Q.—How much does the State of Florida spend a year on roads?
Figures for the fiscal year 1962-63 indicate that approximately
$200 million was spent on engineering, purchase of right of way,
maintenance, and construction of State-maintained facilities in Florida. This included revenue from the seven-cents State gasoline tax,
federal aid, and county bond issues backed by the pledge of surplus
secondary gas tax. [Chairman, Road Department]

Q.—How much do the 67 counties spend on roads?
Revenue from the secondary gas tax (fifth, sixth, and seventh cents)
amounted to $45 million. In addition, secondary bond programs
backed by the pledge of surplus secondary gas tax amounted to $43
million. These figures, for the fiscal year 1962-63, are representative
of the recent years. [Chairman, Road Department]

*Q.—How much does the federal government spend on roads in
Florida?*
Federal aid received during the fiscal year 1962-63 totaled $57 mil-
lion. [Chairman, Road Department]

*Q.—What roads does the State pay for? the federal government?
counties?*
The State finances the construction of the primary State-maintained
system and pays its share of the costs of the Interstate system with
the first four cents of the seven-cents gas tax. In Florida a motorist
pays a gas tax of eleven cents a gallon. The federal government receives four cents of this tax and returns it to the State for the construction of the Interstate superhighways and also contributes a portion to help finance primary and secondary road projects. The 67
counties receive three cents from each gallon of gasoline to construct
the secondary highway network. [Chairman, Road Department]

Q.—Is there a formula for dividing out the State's road money?
The State supports its highway activities from earnings of the tax of seven cents a gallon on gasoline and other motor fuels. The allocation of the proceeds of this tax falls into two categories, called "primary" and "secondary" funds.

Primary money consists of the yield from four cents of the tax. This money is for the unrestricted use of the State Road Department, with the portion used for new construction being allocated on what the SRD calls a "sufficiency rating" of the entire main road system.

Secondary money, the yield from the remaining three cents of the fuel tax, is distributed among the counties on a formula of area, population, and pre-1931 contribution to the State road construction. This money is used to build and maintain roads and bridges, and to pay principal and interest requirements of bonds issued for the same purposes.

Q.—What are primary roads?
So far as the public is concerned, a primary road is one which provides a minimum of two 13-foot traffic lanes. The Road Department has an additional identification for its purposes: a primary road is one whose construction and maintenance is paid from the proceeds of the unearmarked four cents of the State tax on gasoline and other motor fuels.

Q.—What are secondary roads?
The motoring public finds the traffic lanes on these roads range from nine to twelve feet in width. Generally, these roads are intended to serve fewer cars than primary highways. Secondary roads have another meaning to the State Road Department, for their construction and maintenance is paid from the three cents of the State gasoline and motor fuels tax earmarked for use in specific counties. The amount each county receives is determined by a formula which has for its factors the county's area, population, and pre-1931 contribution to the State's highway system.

Q.—Who appoints the Road Board?
The Road Board is appointed by the Governor and serves at his pleasure. The terms of the Board members run concurrent with that of the Governor. [Chairman, Road Department]

Q.—Who decides where roads and highways will be built?
Several factors are considered before any facility is built on new

location. Existing traffic patterns indicate the need for a new facility. Traffic and planning engineers make an "origin and destination study" to determine the best location for any new facility. After this determination has been made, public hearings are held to give the general public an opportunity to endorse or reject the proposed new facility. In instances where federal funds are involved public hearings are required by law. [Chairman, Road Department]

Q.—Are members of the State Road Board answerable to anyone besides the Governor?
The Governor has the sole power to appoint and remove members of the State Road Board. In this sense members of the State Road Board are answerable only to the Governor. [Attorney General]

Q.—Are Road Board members "czars" in their districts?
The Board member is the policy maker for the Road Department from the area he represents. The Board as a group makes statewide policy in the administration of the over-all operation of the department. Because there are more roads to be built and maintained than there is money to do these jobs, the board member is a "czar" in the sense of possessing considerable leeway in the exercise of discretion. He will, of course, be influenced in using that discretion by his own regard for public opinion, the wishes of the Governor, and the advice of the department's technicians. As a candidate, the Governor well may have indicated he would adhere to a community's table of priorities for the construction of highways in its area. The Board member likely will be influenced by the Governor's commitment.

Q.—Do Road Board members get a salary?
Board members are paid $6,000 a year.

Q.—Is all road work done on bids?
All major construction and improvements to the State-maintained highway system are completed after competitive bidding by private contractors. Limited improvements to parking areas, etc., are sometimes performed by maintenance forces of the State Road Department. [Chairman, Road Department]

Q.—Can any contractor bid on a road job?
Contractors who qualify by their professional ability and financial stability are eligible to bid on State-financed road projects. Contractors who meet these qualifications are placed on an "approved

contractors" list and notified when State-financed road projects are advertised for bids. [Chairman, Road Department]

Q.—Why are so many road contracts let at one time?
Approximately 300 contractors and suppliers attend the monthly bid lettings in Tallahassee. The average letting includes 20 to 25 projects. If individual lettings were held for each project, it would require the contractors and suppliers to make more than 250 trips a year to Tallahassee to bid on this State work. [Chairman, Road Department]

Q.—If a road contractor doesn't finish a road on time, is he punished?
A contractor who fails to finish a project on time suffers a financial loss not to exceed $300 a day. The money he loses amounts to one-fourth of one per cent of the total contract each day he is delinquent. A contractor who is delinquent on a project is not eligible to bid on other State work until that project has been completed. [Chairman, Road Department]

Q.—If a property owner refuses to sell land for a right of way, what happens?
State law allows the Road Department to condemn land if the property owner refuses to sell the land for a highway. The State assumes all court expenses for the landowner in such cases. [Chairman, Road Department]

Q.—What is eminent domain?
Eminent domain is the power of the State to take private property for public use. The Florida Constitution, in Section 12 of the Declaration of Rights, provides that no private property may be taken without just compensation. The Legislature has provided generally, in Chapters 73 and 74, Florida Statutes, the procedure to be followed in the exercise of the right of eminent domain by the State or any of its subdivisions, Section 73.13 specifically providing for the payment of compensation for property taken through the exercise of such power. [Attorney General]

Q.—Why do people get so much money for the land they sell the State for right of way?
A person who is not satisfied with the State appraisal for the value of his property is guaranteed his "day in court." The court and jury then decide the final value of his land. The "so much money" is determined by the court. [Chairman, Road Department]

Q.—Does anyone ever give the State the land for a highway?
On limited occasions private individuals have given right of way to the State at no cost. [Chairman, Road Department]

Q.—Who appraises the land values for road right of way?
Land values are appraised by private appraisers hired by the Road Department. The Road Department appraisers review and approve or deny these appraisals. [Chairman, Road Department]

Q.—How wide is the right of way for Florida highways?
The width of the right of way depends upon the nature of the facility. A four-lane primary route requires a 100-foot right of way while rural Interstate superhighways require a 300-foot right of way. [Chairman, Road Department]

Q.—Who buys the rights of way for new roads, counties or State?
The State and federal governments combine finances to purchase rights of way for the Interstate system. Counties purchase rights of way with secondary gas tax funds for primary and secondary roads. [Chairman, Road Department]

Q.—Does the right of way ever cost more than the cost of construction?
In urban areas right-of-way costs often exceed the cost of construction. This situation exists because urban real estate usually has been highly developed commercially. The Department must purchase and remove all improvements on the right of way before construction can begin. Rural right of way is considerably less expensive. [Chairman, Road Department]

Q.—Is it true that the smaller counties have more road money than they need, while the larger counties don't have enough?
Because of the ever increasing traffic volume throughout the state, no county in recent years has found itself with more road money than could be properly spent. Because of the higher cost of urban right of way, counties with large municipal areas find improvements to city traffic facilities exceedingly expensive. [Chairman, Road Department]

Q.—Do cities have to pay for all road and street improvements inside the city limits?
Cities do not pay for the construction or improvement of any street which is included in the State-maintained system. [Chairman, Road Department]

Q.—If a group of citizens don't like the route of a new highway, can they get it changed?

A public hearing is held before the location of a new road is determined. This gives the general public an opportunity to express its approval of a new facility. Once the location has been determined and construction has been started, the location of the new route is not subject to change. [Chairman, Road Department]

Q.—Is it legal to hitchhike on Florida highways?

Yes and no. On regular highways the hitchhiker may thumb a ride legally so long as he stands off the pavement. However, he cannot do this on limited-access roads—Interstate routes and the Turnpike being examples of these—because no pedestrian may lawfully come within the fenced-off rights of way of such express highways.

Q.—How many toll roads, bridges, and ferries are there in Florida?

Toll facilities operated in Florida by the State, counties, and private charter are:

State Operated Facilities

A. Operated by the State Road Department of Florida
    1. Toll roads
        a. Airport Expressway Toll Facility, Miami
        b. Buccaneer Trail, Fernandina Beach
    2. Toll bridges
        a. Emory L. Bennett Causeway to Cape Kennedy
        b. Jacksonville Expressway:
            (1) John E. Mathews Bridge
            (2) Fuller Warren Bridge
            (3) Trout River Bridge
        c. Navarre Bridge over Santa Rosa Sound, Navarre
        d. Pinellas Bayway Toll Facility, St. Petersburg Beach
        e. Sunshine Skyway Toll Facility, St. Petersburg
    3. Toll ferry
        a. Blackbeard and Buccaneer Vessels operating between Mayport and Fort George Island
B. Operated by the Florida State Turnpike Authority
    1. Turnpike
        a. Sunshine State Parkway between Miami and Wildwood
C. Operated by the Santa Rosa Island Authority (Escambia County Agency)
    1. Toll bridge

    a. Pensacola Beach Bridge, Pensacola Beach

COUNTY OPERATED FACILITIES

A. Toll bridges
1. Belleair Beach Causeway, Belleair to Belleair Beach (operated by Pinellas County)
2. Sanibel Causeway (operated by Lee County, linking Sanibel and Captiva Islands to the mainland)
3. Venetian Causeway, Miami to Miami Beach (operated by Dade Port Authority)
4. Rickenbacker Causeway, Miami to Biscayne Key (operated by Metropolitan Dade County)

CITY OPERATED FACILITIES

A. Toll bridges
1. Broad Causeway, Bay Harbor Island
2. Clearwater Pass Toll Bridge, Clearwater
3. Treasure Island Causeway, Treasure Island

PRIVATELY OPERATED FACILITIES

A. Toll bridges
1. Boca Grande Toll Facility, from Placida to Gasparilla Island (operated by the Florida Bridge Company in Charlotte County)

B. Ferries
1. St. George Island Ferry, operating between East Point and St. George Island (operated by the St. George Island Gulf Beaches, Incorporated, and subsidized by the State Road Department and Franklin County)
2. Dog Island Ferry, operating between Carrabelle and Dog Island (operated by the Dog Island Company and subsidized by the State Road Department and Franklin County)

[Director, Revenue Projects Division, Road Department]

Q.—Can I picnic anywhere on the highway right of way?
Motorists are allowed to picnic on the State-maintained right of way except on the Interstate routes and Sunshine State Parkway where such activity is prohibited. The State Road Department has constructed more than 200 wayside parks along the primary and secondary road networks to accommodate motorists who desire to picnic. However, motorists who picnic in areas other than wayside parks must remove their vehicles far enough away from the traffic lanes to avoid creating a traffic hazard. [Chairman, Road Department]

Q.—What is the Turnpike?

The Turnpike is a 256-mile limited-access toll road extending from Wildwood in Central Florida to Miami in South Florida. The original 109-mile portion of this facility was opened to traffic in 1957, and the remaining distance was completed in three portions, the final link being opened to traffic in January, 1964. [Chairman, Road Department]

Q.—Do tolls completely pay the cost of building and maintaining a turnpike?

In the case of the Sunshine State Parkway, the toll road stretching between Miami and Wildwood, revenue from tolls and concessions was pledged to pay off the bonds sold to provide the money to construct the highway. Analysts believe this income will be ample to meet the principal and interest requirements of the debt and to defray the continuing maintenance cost.

Q.—What is an expressway? a freeway?

An expressway is identified as an urban limited-access facility. A freeway is a limited-access facility through rural areas. [Chairman, Road Department]

Q.—What is an expressway authority?

An expressway authority is generally a body politic and corporate and an agency of the State. The duties, jurisdiction, and responsibility of an expressway authority are provided by law. Jurisdiction is limited to a certain area of the state and the purposes and powers, generally, are to construct, improve, maintain, and operate certain expressway systems within a given area. [Attorney General]

Q.—What is the Skyway?

In Florida, those who speak of the Skyway are likely referring to the Sunshine Skyway, a 15.1-mile bridge and causeway toll combination spanning Tampa Bay from St. Petersburg. Its high-level bridge is 4 miles long and rises 15 stories above the water. Under its span pass ocean-going vessels calling at Port Tampa. The Skyway's 11 miles of Gulf beaches offer recreational areas for fishing, boating, swimming, and picnicking.

Q.—Is the present plan to "free" all toll bridges and highways eventually?

Each bond indenture determines the length of indebtedness for each toll project. There is no uniform date for removing tolls from all the facilities in Florida. Also, the Road Department does not supervise all toll facilities; some are operated by private interests. [Chairman, Road Department]

Q.—What is the Interstate system?
The Interstate Highway System is a nationwide network of multi-laned, limited-access type highways. This network of superhighways will crisscross the 48 states in such a manner as to enable a motorist to travel either from East to West or North to South across the entire country without encountering a traffic signal or a grade intersection. This network at present is limited to a total of 41,000 miles by law. Since the beginning of the Interstate program these highways have been designed and constructed to carry as safely as possible the number of vehicles, projected by estimate, that will use them through the year 1975. At the present, consideration is being given to raising design standards to take care of projected traffic use to the year 1985. The number of travel lanes designed and constructed may vary according to projected traffic use in a given location.

Florida has been allocated 1,126 miles of Interstate highways. These miles have been assigned to Interstate Routes 4, 10, 75, and 95. Interstate Route 4 is the only one of these that does not continue into an adjoining state. This highway originates in the Pinellas/Tampa Bay area and goes northeasterly across Florida to its intersection with Interstate Route 95 west of Daytona Beach. Interstate Route 10 will originate in the Jacksonville vicinity and go west through the entire northern area of Florida to the Alabama line. Interstate Route 75 at present will go from the Tampa vicinity north through the central area of Florida to the Georgia line. Interstate Route 95 will go from the Miami vicinity north, paralleling the Atlantic Coast, to the Georgia line. [Interstate Administrator, Road Department]

Q.—Who builds the Interstate Highway System?
The Interstate Highway System is being constructed by the individual states under the supervision of the United States Bureau of Public Roads. [Interstate Administrator, Road Department]

Q.—Who pays for the Interstate Highway System?
This highway system is being paid for in the following manner: Total cost, including engineering, right-of-way acquisition, and construction is paid by 90 per cent from federal funds and 10 per cent

from State funds. The total cost of this interstate system throughout the nation is estimated to be $41 billion. [Interstate Administrator, Road Department]

Q.—Why aren't all United States highways four-laned?
United States routes are not all four-laned because traffic volume will not warrant construction of multi-laned facilities on all routes bearing United States numbers. In Florida, many of the state numbered routes carry heavier traffic loads than some of the United States numbered routes. [Chairman, Road Department]

Q.—Are there any regulations affecting the pulling of house trailers on the highway?
There are five regulations.

1. A special permit must be obtained from the State Road Department to pull house trailers over eight feet in width.

2. The speed limit for vehicles pulling house trailers is 50 miles per hour in the daytime and 45 at night, with the exception of limited-access routes (Interstate system only) where the limit is 60 mph and 55 at night, with an absolute 40-mph minimum speed.

3. Safety chains shall be attached from the vehicle to the trailer and shall be of sufficient strength to maintain connection of the trailer to the pulling vehicle under all conditions.

4. No persons shall occupy a house trailer while it is being moved on a public highway.

5. House trailers in excess of 80 inches in width shall be required to have clearance lamps, turn signal lights, and stop lights, as well as the proper reflectors, and shall carry emergency flares for breakdown purposes.
[Director, Department of Public Safety]

Q.—Does the State regulate billboards along the highways?
The Management and Disposal branch of the Right-of-Way Division of the State Road Department regulates outdoor advertising along the State-maintained highway system. Signs are prohibited within fifteen feet of the State-maintained right of way outside municipal limits. Within municipal limits, advertisements may be erected adjacent to the right of way. [Chairman, Road Department]

Q.—Is the State liable for accidents caused by potholes in the highways?
The State is not liable for accidents caused by potholes in the high-

ways. The Road Department erects signs identifying any substandard segments on the State-maintained system and posts speed limits compatible with these road conditions. [Chairman, Road Department]

Q.—Is the litterbug law in Florida enforced?
The Florida Highway Patrol is charged with enforcing the law regarding litterbugging. [Chairman, Road Department]

Q.—What are some of Florida's most famous bridges?
Some of Florida's most famous bridges include the series of structures linking Key West with the mainland identified as the Overseas Highway, the Sunshine Skyway across lower Tampa Bay, the Pensacola Bay Bridge on U. S. 90 (this $8 million bridge represents the largest single structure ever awarded by the State Road Department), the John E. Mathews Bridge across the St. Johns River in Jacksonville, the Howard Frankland Bridge on Interstate Route 4 across Tampa Bay, and the Shands Bridge across the St. Johns River near Green Cove Springs linking Clay and St. Johns Counties. A new concrete bridge was completed in 1962 at Green Cove Springs replacing the old Shands Bridge, which was the longest wooden structure in the world. [Chairman, Road Department]

Q.—Are there any detailed road maps of Florida counties available? Where?
Detailed road maps of Florida counties can be obtained by writing the Supply Unit, State Road Department, Holland Building, Tallahassee, Florida. A price list is available for those interested in purchasing these maps. [Chairman, Road Department]

Learning More
About Florida

*Q.—What books or other publications are available, from publishers
or libraries, that might help me learn more about people in
Florida?*

Dust Tracks on a Road, an Autobiography, by Zora Neale Hurston.
1942.

 Fabulous Hoosier, by Jane W. Fisher. 1947.

 Florida's Flagler, by S. Walter Martin. 1949.

 *'Gaters, Skeeters, and Malary; Recollections of a Pioneer Florida
Judge*, by E. C. May. 1953.

 The Legendary Mizners, by Alva Johnston. 1953.

 Napoleon Bonaparte Broward, Florida's Fighting Democrat, by
Samuel Proctor. 1950.

 *A Prince in Their Midst; the Adventurous Life of Achille Murat
on the American Frontier*, by A. J. Hanna. 1946.

 Stephen R. Mallory, Confederate Navy Chief, by Joseph T. Dur-
kin. 1954.

 The World Grows Round My Door, by David G. Fairchild. 1947.

 A Yank Pioneer in Florida, by Allen H. Andrews. 1950.

. . . about Florida cookery?

Cross Creek Cookery, by Marjorie Kinnan Rawlings. 1942.

 The Gasparilla Cookbook, by The Junior League of Tampa. 1961.

 The Key West Cook Book, by the Members of the Key West
Woman's Club. 1949.

 Trade Winds Cookery; Tropical Recipes for All America, by
Norma A. Davis. 1956.

. . . about Florida description and travel?

Cross Creek, by Marjorie Kinnan Rawlings. 1942.

Florida: A Guide to the Southernmost State, compiled and written by the Federal Writers' Project. 1939.

Florida: A Way of Life, by Mike (Mrs. Tom Q.) Smith. 1960.

Florida: Land of Fortune, by Stephen J. Flynn. 1962.

Gateway to Space, by Charles I. Coombs. 1961.

Jonathan Dickinson's Journal, or God's Protecting Providence, edited by Evangeline Walker Andrews and Charles McLean Andrews. 1945.

Palmetto Country, by Stetson Kennedy. 1942.

Suwannee River; Strange Green Land, by Cecile Hulse Matschat. 1938.

The Travels of William Bartram, edited by Francis Harper. 1958.

... about Florida gardening?

500 Answers to Your Florida Garden Questions, by Herbert S. Wolfe, John V. Watkins, and Thomas B. Mack. 1957.

Florida Gardening, Month by Month, by Nixon Smiley. 1957.

Fruits for Southern Florida, by David Sturrock. 1959.

Gardening in the Lower South, by H. H. Hume. 1954.

Subtropical Gardening in Florida, by Nixon Smiley. 1951.

Your Florida Garden, by John V. Watkins and Herbert S. Wolfe. 1956.

Your Guide to Florida Landscape Plants: Palms, Trees, Shrubs, Vines, by John V. Watkins. 1961.

... about Florida history?

The Everglades: River of Grass, by Marjory Stoneman Douglas. 1947.

Flight into Oblivion, by A. J. Hanna. 1938.

Florida During the Territorial Days, by S. Walter Martin. 1944.

Florida, Land of Change, by Kathryn T. Abbey Hanna. 1948.

Florida, the Land of Romance, by Dorothy Dodd. 1956.

Florida Under Five Flags, by Rembert W. Patrick. 1960.

Florida's Golden Sands, by Alfred Jackson Hanna and Kathryn Abbey Hanna. 1950.

How to Win in Politics, by Fuller Warren. 1948.

Journey into Wilderness, by Jacob Rhett Motte, edited by James F. Sunderman. 1953.

The Key to the Golden Islands, by Carita Doggett Corse. 1931.

Lake Okeechobee, Wellspring of the Everglades, by Alfred Jackson Hanna and Kathryn Abbey Hanna. 1948.

Lore of the Wreckers, by Birse Shepard. 1961.

The St. Johns, a Parade of Diversities, by Branch Cabell and A. J. Hanna. 1943.

...about Florida natural history?

Adventures with Reptiles; the Story of Ross Allen, by Clarence Hylander. 1951.

American Seashells, by R. Tucker Abbott. 1954.

Common Exotic Trees of South Florida, by Mary Franklin Barrett. 1956.

Eagle Man; Charles L. Broley's Field Adventures with American Eagles, by Myrtle Jeanne Broley. 1952.

Field Guide to the Shells of Our Atlantic and Gulf Coasts, by Percy A. Morris. 1951.

Flight into Sunshine, Bird Experiences in Florida, by Helen G. Cruickshank. 1948.

Florida Bird Life, by Arthur H. Howell. 1932.

Florida Bird Life, by Alexander Sprunt. 1954.

Florida Wild Flowers, by Mary Francis Baker. 1938.

Guide to the Reptiles, Amphibians, and Fresh-water Fishes of Florida, by Archie Carr and Coleman J. Goin. 1955.

The Native Trees of Florida, by Erdman West and Lillian E. Arnold. 1956.

That Vanishing Eden, a Naturalist's Florida, by Thomas Barbour. 1944.

World Outside My Door, by Olive Brown Goin. 1955.

...about Florida government?

The Florida Handbook, compiled by Allen Morris, revised and republished biennially. (School libraries, generally)

Our Florida Government, by Allen Morris, 1961. (State-adopted textbook)

A Guide for Visitors to the House of Representatives, a short course in lawmaking, available free from the Office of the Speaker, House of Representatives, The Capitol, Tallahassee.

The Supreme Court of Florida, a pamphlet containing basic information about the court and its home, available free from the Office of the Chief Justice, the Supreme Court, Tallahassee.

...about Florida, generally?

Atlas of Florida, by Erwin Raisz and John R. Dunkle. 1964.

Criminal Court of Record, 53
"Crippled child," defined, 34
Crippled Children's Commission, 34, 35

DEATH PENALTY, 64, 65
Dental college, 86
Dependent children, aid to, 113
Detectives, private, 67, 68
Development Commission, 35
Disabled persons, tax exemption, 103
District Courts of Appeal, 53
Divorce: records, 109; requirements, 108, 109
Driver's licenses, 106, 107

EDUCATION, Board of, 82
Elections, 73
Eminent domain, defined, 128
Equalization, tax, boards of, 99
"Equal rights" amendment, ratification by Florida, 9
Everglades, origin of name, 12, 13
Expressway, defined, 132
Extradition, power of Governor, 35

FBI, in Florida, 68
Federal: courts, 60; occupation of Florida, 8
"Filled land," defined, 89
Fish, purchase from State hatchery, 119
Fishing: regulation of, 118, 119, 122; game fish, defined, 123; sale of salt-water fish, 122; salt-water closed seasons, 122, 123
Flag, State, 9
Flags, five over Florida, 1
Florida: acquisition from Spain, 4; admission to Union, 6; British rule, 3; in Civil War, 8; federal occupation, 8; first settlement, 1; French settlement, 2; naming of, 1; permanent settlement, 1; ratification of Fourteenth Amendment, 9; Spanish rule, 2; State flag, 9; territorial government, 4, 5; the 13 Colonies, 4; vote on statehood, 6
Florida Keys, number of, 93
Florida products, commissions to encourage use of, 34
Floridians, origin of, 6, 7
"Floridians" or "Floridans," 6
Flood control districts, 93
Flower, State, 13
Foster, Stephen Collins, 13
Fourteenth Amendment, ratification, 9
Freeholder, definition of, 73

Freeway, defined, 132
French settlement, 2

GAME FISH, defined, 123
General revenue fund, 96
Governor: appointments by, 32; compensation, 31; death of, 32; death penalty, 65; duties of, 18, 19; extradition powers, 35; how to write, 31; inability to serve, 32; mansion, 32; patronage, 28, 31, 32; press conferences, 31; qualifications to run, 71, 72; resignation of, 32; veto powers, 40; youngest, 33
Grand juries, 56, 57
Groynes, defined, 90
Gun permits, 118

HIGHWAY PATROL AUTHORITY, 67
Highways. See Roads
Historical collections, 12
Historic sites, protection of, 86
Hitchhiking, 130
Homestead exemption, 101, 102
Hotel and Restaurant Commission, 25, 26
House trailers, regulation of, 134
Hunting: animals hunted year-round, 118; areas, public, 117; licenses, 116, 117; protected birds, 117; seasons, 116

IMPEACHMENTS, 47, 48
Indictments, 57
Inspection services, 27, 28
Internal Improvement Fund, Trustees of, 88, 89
Interstate Highway System, 133

JACKSON, Andrew, 4
Journals, legislative, 44
Judges: qualifications of, 52; selection of, 51
Junior colleges: admission standards, 84; enrollment at, 84; in State school systems, 85
Jury service, 55, 56
Justice of Peace Courts, 54
"Just value," 100

KEYS, number of Florida, 93

LAND, State-owned, 88
Law enforcement officers, kinds of, 66
Law schools, 86
Laws: effective date, 41, 42; local, 42; number existing, 39; number passed, 39

PB-10-25